Sunset

COTTAGE
STYLE decorating

BY CYNTHIA BIX AND THE EDITORS OF SUNSET BOOKS

Sunset Books ❦ Menlo Park, California

SUNSET BOOKS

VICE PRESIDENT, GENERAL MANAGER:
Richard A. Smeby

VICE PRESIDENT, EDITORIAL DIRECTOR:
Bob Doyle

PRODUCTION DIRECTOR:
Lory Day

DIRECTOR OF OPERATIONS:
Rosann Sutherland

RETAIL SALES
DEVELOPMENT MANAGER:
Linda Barker

ART DIRECTOR:
Vasken Guiragossian

STAFF FOR THIS BOOK

DEVELOPMENTAL EDITOR:
Linda J. Selden

COPY EDITOR:
Phyllis Elving

PHOTO DIRECTOR/STYLIST:
JoAnn Masaoka Van Atta

DESIGN:
Alice Rogers

PRODUCTION ASSISTANCE:
Linda Bouchard

PRINCIPAL PHOTOGRAPHER:
Jamie Hadley

PRODUCTION COORDINATOR:
Danielle Javier

PROOFREADER:
Mary Roybal

COTTAGE COMFORTS

If visions of a bright and airy seaside cottage or a cozy country village dwelling make you yearn for simple comforts, this book is for you. Cottage-style decorating is all about creating that kind of comfort and intimacy in your own home, whatever its location or vintage.

Today's fresh cottage style is flexible—it borrows the best from modest dwellings of past and present, country and lakeside, home and abroad, and melds them into a look and atmosphere that are highly personal as well as lovely to look at. This delightful style takes all the elements that make home a pleasant place to be—casual furnishings, engaging colors and patterns, simple spaces open to light and air—and spices them with a liberal dash of imagination to create living spaces that are sophisticated yet warmly welcoming.

In preparing this book, we were fortunate to work with the owners of many beautiful cottage-style homes; we'd like to thank all of them for their generosity in opening up their homes for us to photograph.

10 9 8

First printing March 2003

ISBN 0-376-01108-4
Library of Congress Control Number: 2002115937
Printed in the United States of America

For additional copies of *Cottage Style Decorating* or any other Sunset book, see our web site at www.sunsetbooks.com or call 1-800-526-5111.

CONTENTS

COVER: Sunny colors, casual furniture, and one-of-a-kind personal touches—this living-dining space embodies the relaxed, upbeat essence of cottage style.

DESIGN: Molly English/Camps and Cottages.
CABINET DESIGN: Steve Reed.
PHOTOGRAPHY: Jamie Hadley.
COVER DESIGN: Vasken Guiragossian.
PHOTO DIRECTION: JoAnn Masaoka Van Atta.

FRESH COTTAGE STYLE

FOR SOME PEOPLE, THE WORD "COTTAGE" summons up fairy-tale images of thatched-roof dwellings in the English countryside, or quaint little homes of rough-hewn stone nestled in the woods. For others it evokes a picture of a white-shingled getaway at the seashore, a log cabin by the lake, or even a little farmhouse in France. Whatever comes to mind for you, all such dwellings share some important basic qualities: a sense of modest scale, a special feeling of coziness and welcome, an air of unassuming informality. "Cottage" is the essence of what we think of as home.

Today, happily, we need not live out in the countryside or in a one-room dwelling to live in country cottage style. Cottage style can be created in any home, new or old, where an unpretentious, individual spirit is allowed its expression in furnishings, colors, and accessories. ❦ While cottage style is really an extension of American country style, encompassing the expansiveness of a classic country barn as well as the intimacy of a vacation cabin, it also borrows from the charming traditions of the French Provincial, English cottage, and even Swedish country looks. And though it takes elements from a range of design "eras," from the elegant simplicity of 19th-century Shaker style to the bright primary motifs of the 1940s and the more recent "shabby-chic" look, it recombines them to form something quite contemporary. Fresh cottage style mixes the antique and vintage with the brand-new, the classic with the rustic, the traditional with the unexpected. ❦ Today's cottage style has a light and airy quality—a happy marriage of simple, unfussy spaces and a feeling of openness to the outdoors. A cottage-style room may feature many elements, such as collectible treasures or a lighthearted mix of patterns and motifs, but the look isn't cluttered. Rather, it's unified by color, theme, or the style of its components. And it's brightened with light walls and wood-work, and plenty of natural light streaming in. ❦ Perhaps, in the end, cottage style is really a state of mind. It's about the handmade and the homemade— objects crafted and selected with loving care and individual flair. It's about simplicity, and a connection with nature. It's about color and texture—ocean blue and cornfield green, rough-sawn wood and gleaming fired clay. And it's about combining beauty with economy and practicality, as evidenced in the pleasing shape of a ceramic water pitcher or the rainbow colors of a rug created from leftover fabric scraps. Most of all, it's about your own highly per-sonal way of expressing what "home" means to you.

COTTAGE ROOMS

Upstairs, downstairs, all around the house—every room, from your front entry to your bedroom sanctuary, takes on a uniquely comfortable air when you give it a touch of fresh cottage style. Brightly painted chairs around your dining table, a collection of baskets atop a cabinet, crisp checked curtains above the kitchen sink—all convey that easy cottage spirit.

For public areas such as entryways, living rooms, and dining rooms, you'll find a great range of furniture (from rustic cabin to shabby-chic), lighting, and accessories with cottage style. A classic country cottage kitchen can be created with elements as grand as a vintage range or as small as a collection of salt-and-pepper shakers. In bedrooms and baths, cottage ambience is lent with linens and lots of little touches. Even porches, sunrooms, and tucked-away nooks can take on a cottage feel. In this chapter, you'll find ideas for cottage style throughout your home.

COMING AND GOING

WHETHER YOUR FAMILY

and friends tend to be front-door or back-door folks, your entry sets the tone for your private world. In a cottage-style house, front hallways and back-door mudrooms can say "home, sweet home" each time someone steps through your door. ❦ Suggest cottage style with a simple pine console table or with an old milk can ready to receive umbrellas. Plants and flowers in baskets, vases, or pitchers make for a charming indoor-outdoor connection. Cottage-style accessories, from straw hats to antique garden tools, help convey an impression of casual simplicity. And a display of artwork—paintings, photos, folk-art pieces, even vintage advertising signs—bestows cottage personality. ❦ Don't forget the practicalities—a place to park your walking stick or your book, or perhaps a bench where you can sit to pull off boots. Guests will appreciate a mirror for a quick touch-up, along with hooks or a hall tree for jackets or hats.

JUST A FEW ELEMENTS can neatly define your entryway and establish a distinctive decorating style at the same time. Here, a vintage "shabby-chic" tone is set with a one-of-a-kind hat rack fashioned from a piece of old molding and antique doorknobs. Hung with romantic straw hats and a vintage reticule, it's right in keeping with the antique garden chair and little table beneath.

KEEPING IT SIMPLE can be the best course for a small entry area like this one, where an understated color scheme conveys restful warmth. A pine-framed mirror, a muslin-skirted table with wooden box ready to receive keys, and an antique bread basket for walking sticks or umbrellas are pretty and useful. Unexpected personal touches include the softly glowing glass lamp and the plates framing the mirror, hinting at the owners' passion for vintage china.

TOUCHES OF COUNTRIFIED ELEGANCE—*a white upholstered chair and a lovely French-style "trumeau" mirror with decorative panel—mix easily with such down-to-earth elements as a vintage lead potting table and plants in simple containers. The result is a fresh and welcoming atmosphere for this garden entrance. A curtain hanging just inside the French doors adds a grace note.*

WITH SUCH ARTFULLY ARRANGED ELEMENTS, *this entryway could be the
subject for a still-life painting. The focal point—a vintage poster—rests casually
atop the weathered table, its rectangular outline offset by an exuberant cluster
of hats and dangling string bags. Anchoring the scene are a pail of lush feverfew,
a pair of candlesticks, grasses in a trio of terra-cotta pots, and an old stool.*

THIS ENTRYWAY TABLEAU makes the most of a wooden bench, a scattering of pillows, and a delightful barn cupboard. Bench and cupboard were created from recycled redwood, painted to give an appearance of age. The pillows are covered in a retro 1940s tropical print on barkcloth. The real vintage pieces? A painted basket and a cast-iron dog doorstop. Below, an old English wooden "firkin" holds kindling from outdoors.

SHAKER-LIKE SIMPLICITY informs this arresting contemporary entry—in spirit, if not in actual stylistic details. The unadorned walls, with their soaring angles and soft contrasting colors, play off the darker hues and solid form of the oversize painting, to dramatic effect. Matched topiaries contribute a touch of greenery without adding any clutter to the scene.

BEING TOGETHER

THE HEART OF YOUR HOME is anyplace people gather to talk, celebrate, share a meal, or just take it easy. Whether that is a living room, a family room, an informal dining room, or a "great room" that combines all three, a relaxed approach to furnishings and decor expresses a warm sense of hospitality. ❦ In living areas, the emphasis is on easy comfort. Seating should be flexible, allowing you to pull up an extra chair for a guest or to gather around a game table. Provide no-fuss footrests and side tables for books and cups. Let sunlight flood in by day, and combine soft lighting with practical reading lamps for nighttime. In summer, dress furniture in light slipcovers; in winter, provide fleecy throws for snuggling on chilly evenings. ❦ A dining room can take on an informal cottage air with the right furniture, lighting fixtures, and accessories. Choose a farm table and mismatched chairs or even a park bench, display an eclectic collection of dishes in a hutch, and put fresh flowers everywhere.

THIS SUNNY LIVING SPACE *exudes comfortable country cottage style. In the breakfast nook, a window seat wraps around a pine table below striped cotton window shades and a collection of ironstone dishware marching along a handsome bracketed plate rail. The sitting room's soft green and off-white palette, accented with red touches, is offered in an appealingly casual mix of fabric patterns.*

A CAPACIOUS antique Irish bed cupboard—an early version of the Murphy bed—now houses a television and audio equipment in this cozy seating area off the kitchen/breakfast room. The original green paint has aged to a lovely patina. On top, a collection of American baskets, along with an antique birdcage, softens the cupboard's lines.

A REAL CONVERSATION PIECE, this grouping of vintage miniature furniture from England may have been made as a salesman's model. Now it graces the rustic console tabletop behind the sofa, creating a witty juxtaposition of scale. The antique Windsor chair shown at left still has its original paint, picturesquely distressed by age.

BRASS CANDLESTICKS of varied heights make an attractive grouping atop an antique apothecary cabinet. At left, a painted wood fireplace mantel is a reproduction in classic style. The balanced, symmetrical arrangement of ironstone pieces and twin topiaries atop the mantel carries out the traditional look, as does the antique portrait.

THIS ANTIQUE Georgian corner cupboard has a handsome restored surface that was actually the result of careful hand-stripping and application of a new exterior finish. The original green paint was left on the interior, making an effective backdrop for the owner's collection of English and American ironstone.

IT'S ALL OF A PIECE—*an antique pine dining table blending perfectly with reproduction chairs in wheat-sheaf design as well as a magnificent antique pine hutch. Dominating the room, the hutch shows off a fine collection of majolica—distinctively glazed earthenware featuring shapes and motifs from nature.*

OLD AND NEW, *from Asia and North America—the eclectic furnishings in the home featured on these two pages express the owners' finely honed tastes, resulting in a serene, contemplative dwelling among the trees. A comfortable new sofa pulls up to a vintage Tibetan prayer chest; a time-softened Oriental carpet underlies an old English pedestal table in a living room that's an oasis of soothing white walls amid surrounding greenery.*

AT ONE END OF THE ROOM, *a venerable fireplace of picturesque, uneven clinker bricks is a place to relax in cozy comfort. Paintings, china figures, and other treasures offer something of interest everywhere one looks.*

VINTAGE WICKER ROCKERS, their cushions upholstered in remnants of old tapestry fabric, flank a new armoire made in the style of 1930s bamboo-and-wood furniture.

SALVAGED from an antebellum home in Georgia, a wooden pillar—one of a pair—graces the opening to the sunroom below. Simple furnishings invite repose while offering a view of greenery and sky. Below right, a Mexican child's chair, still with its original finish, adds a whimsical touch of antique charm.

STENCILING is an easy and inexpensive way to dress up a wall. A delightful handmade look characterizes this cheery border stenciled around a vine-hung patio door. Red and white checks recall the colors and motifs of the 1930s and '40s, celebrated throughout this sunny California bungalow.

THE FINE ART OF DISPLAY is charmingly demonstrated by the corner assemblage pictured above. An old wicker trunk provides storage while functioning as a "table" on which to show off collectible books and a vintage watering can. Atop it all, a whimsical rustic lamp features a bear beneath a "tree" robed in vintage fabric. Note how accessories subtly carry out the room's color palette.

BRIGHT AS A CALIFORNIA SUNSET, a pillow-strewn sofa dominates this sunroom. Uncovered windows let in maximum light and gentle breezes. A rare four-hoop hickory chair, its paint faded to a soft red, adds grace and interest. Behind the sofa, a handmade pond boat from the 1930s was the owner's serendipitous find.

DESIGNED TO EVOKE *that legendary sunny California atmosphere of the 1920s, '30s, and '40s, this living room is awash in light reflected off buttercup-yellow walls. Furnishings in soft greens and cheery reds convey jaunty ease. The cupboard looks antique but is really new, its convincing patina created with no fewer than 33 coats of paint. Around it hang paintings by California artists.*

WARM IN TONE yet light and airy, this dining/family room gains a feeling of space and light through the use of a generously sized mirror set amid built-in maple cabinets on the far wall. New furniture made from vintage light pine, combined with the uncluttered design of the cabinetry, keeps the look up-to-date.

SOFTEST FERN GREEN painted on walls and paired with fresh white in upholstery conveys a sense of serenity in the sitting area of the same room pictured at top. A folding triple mirror from an old dressing table and an antique pine cabinet extend the design theme of the dining area. A judicious selection of Staffordshire china is a lovely personal touch.

DINING BY THE HEARTH is a cozy cottage pleasure of long standing, and this room issues an invitation to continue the tradition. The American Colonial spirit is reflected in everything here, from the aged beam mantel, graceful decoys, and imposing old clock to the polished pine table and finely embellished Windsor chair.

A FRESH BLENDING of the new and the traditional, this dining/sitting room gains old-time country character from the well-worn farmhouse table surrounded by Windsor chairs and dominated by a pair of dramatic hurricane lamps. White-painted walls, wide-open French doors, and light-hued rattan chairs in front of the fireplace leaven the look with contemporary flair.

HEARTH AND HOME

IN THE "GOOD OLD DAYS" BEFORE CENTRAL HEATING, THE HEART OF EVERY HOME WAS ITS HEARTH. Everyone gathered around it to talk and read, stitch and whittle, and even cook. Although a fireplace is no longer our principal source of warmth, treating the hearth as a focal point is a sure-fire way to create a cozy cottage atmosphere. Begin by arranging sofas, chairs, and coffee table closely around your fireplace. You may be fortunate to have a fireplace and mantel that already have old-fashioned character. But even a contemporary fireplace can take on a cottage personality through clever decor touches, as illustrated on these pages.

DRESS-UPS Group nosegays in pottery vases on the mantel, or make your mantel a display shelf for favorite objects. For a casual but pulled-together look, feature one or two large objects or group related smaller things together. Set an arrangement of dried or fresh flowers and foliage in the firebox or on the hearth during times when the fireplace isn't in use; you can also find candelabras specially made for display in your fireplace.

FOR A TOUCH OF COTTAGE STYLE, set a rustic bench by your hearth. Add a large basket to hold firewood and pinecones or fireplace tools, as shown in the photo at right. For evenings, light candles set in wooden holders or glass hurricane chimneys. With simple additions like these, any fireplace setting takes on cottage character. Above, twigs and ivy wrapped around an iron latticework make a charming decoration for an off-duty fireplace.

A FAVORITE PAINTING OR FAMILY PORTRAIT—*or a weathered antique mirror—will draw all eyes to the fireplace. Above, wall-mounted baskets of dried flowers help frame the art over the mantel, while a vintage iron fence section makes a handsome fire screen. Useful accessories include bellows to coax flames from a waning fire (right) and andirons to support logs in the fireplace (far left).*

ELEGANCE, COTTAGE STYLE, *infuses every corner of this tastefully appointed living/dining space. Setting the tone in both rooms are gorgeous folding screens—a good idea for adding interest to corners and for artfully concealing closet doors. The fine French antique dining table is flanked by assorted chairs of 1930s and '40s vintages. Gracing the living room fireplace mantel (right), a French "trumeau" mirror, still with its original paint, is an elegant backdrop for a sleek horse, a French antique carved from fruitwood.*

THE FURNITURE in this dining area—together with the fresh white color and antique ornaments—gives the room a classic, Swedish-inspired look. The owners' son created the handsome cupboard from both old and new elements; similarly, the vintage table base has a new top. Geometric designs painted on the hardwood floor add pizzazz, while black and white furnishings are dramatic against ochre walls.

REFLECTING THE HUES of surf, rock, and sky visible just outside the window, the painted wood furnishings in this fisherman's cottage have a fairy-tale quality that's perfectly in tune with the rustic stone walls. The corner cupboard fancifully frames a collection of brightly patterned dishes.

ONE END *of this cozy living/dining room— furnished with a vintage iron daybed dressed in pale shabby-chic linens, plus a vintage mirror and table—can serve as a mini–guest room. The floral drapes are swung shut and a fabric screen (just visible on the left side) is brought out to enclose the space, creating a private corner.*

A VINTAGE JELLY CUPBOARD *is topped with salvaged pieces that evoke a garden feeling—including green-painted brackets, a piece of decorative lattice hung on the wall, and a vase of hydrangeas from the spectacular shrub gracing the garden just outside the window.*

AT ONE WITH THE GARDEN BEYOND, *this light and airy dining room has as its centerpiece a glass-topped table and chairs—vintage garden furniture. Bearing their original paint, these pieces have been allowed to rust naturally, giving them a genteel, time-worn quality. The room's white and misty-hued furnishings glow in light from full-length windows, creating an ethereal vision.*

COTTAGE KITCHENS

IN AN OLD-FASHIONED cottage home, the kitchen has always been more than just a place to cook. A farm-style table was the traditional gathering place, serving both as a dining table and as a place to roll out cookie dough, create craft projects, and work on the household accounts. ❦ Today's kitchen is more central than ever—furnish it for practicality and comfort, and no one will want to be anywhere else. Use natural wood and light colors, with bright fabric touches at windows, on chair seats, and on tables. Display dishes on open shelving, in plate racks, and in that ultimate country cottage kitchen staple—a hutch. ❦ If you are replacing cabinets, consider the new "unfitted" cabinetry that looks like separate pieces of furniture. Or reface cabinets with cottage-style doors and hardware, or paint them using one of the techniques shown on pages 98–103. You might even want to invest in a vintage stove or a rustic butcher-block island. If space permits, provide an inviting eating spot —even a tiny wooden table and two folding chairs tucked into a corner.

THIS DIMINUTIVE KITCHEN *packs a lot of personality into a little space.*
Simple white cabinets and awning-style windows provide a neutral setting
for an assortment of red-and-white collectibles—canisters, vintage
decorated milk glass, a farmer-boy cookie jar, enamelware, and more.
All are meant to be used as well as admired.

IN THIS TINY COTTAGE, *butter-yellow walls above a white beadboard dado warm an intimate breakfast/sitting room off the kitchen. Varied prints and patterns in red and white—candy stripes, fresh florals, homespun windowpane checks, and the jaunty designs of vintage table linens—harmonize with one another and with folk-art pieces and kitchenware to paint a delightful country-cottage picture. Even the artfully arranged antique china in its white beadboard wall cupboard (right) carries out the color theme. Beneath the shelves, a folk-art piece expresses a favorite country motif—chickens!—that's also evident in artwork hung on the walls, as seen below.*

A CLASSIC ENGLISH FARMHOUSE *look has been created in the kitchen at right, thanks to the talented owner who created its cabinets and teak countertops. A 19th-century salt-glazed water filter jar looks handsome beneath the sink. To unite the spaces of this tiny house, walls are painted white and wide-plank floors of spruce are laid throughout. Oak posts and beams (visible below) were stained to echo the old oak of the 18th-century English furnishings. A vintage cast-iron stove from Connecticut is inscribed thus: "If I am good, please tell others about it."*

WALKING INTO THIS KITCHEN is like stepping back into Merrie Olde England,
though many of the antiques actually have other origins. The butcher block came from
an old Connecticut butcher shop, while the hunting horn hanging from a post is
19th-century German. Forming a cozy seating area reminiscent of a pub, Windsor
chairs face an 18th-century oak settle; its pillows are covered in fabric copied
from a pattern by the great 19th-century English designer William Morris.

A SOPHISTICATED EUROPEAN
cottage look characterizes this
light, bright kitchen; countertops
of old French pavers and a
farmhouse sink help set the
style. Simple white cabinets unify
the look and keep it fresh and
uncluttered; windows can be left
uncovered in this woodsy setting
to let in light and views. A casual
seating area, just visible at left in
the photo above, is shown in
more detail on the facing page.

VINTAGE ACCESSORIES can do much to give any kitchen cottage-style flair. At left, an old fruit stand sign, 1930s and '40s California pottery, a pegged shelf, and other lighthearted accents—all in period green and yellow—do the trick. Above, a scalloped shelf allows placement of favorite ornaments above the sink; a clever eye saw a way to display old silver knives to advantage.

AN ANTIQUE MEXICAN cabinet is the focus of this intimate seating area (part of the kitchen on the facing page). It's open to show off part of the owners' collection of decorative china and pottery; over the cabinet door hang an old altar scarf and a French beaded piece. Friends and family can relax here in comfortable wicker chairs while keeping the cook company.

*A RUSTIC-STYLE
COTTAGE KITCHEN
often calls for casual
open shelving rather
than conventional
enclosed cabinets.
Here, the patterns
and colors of dishes
and glassware on
shelves and counters
are delightfully
decorative. Simple
baskets are fine
for holding utensils.*

*IN A COTTAGE
built of native stone,
a vintage stove
looks right at home.
Such accessories as
the big wall clock
and the rustic
pine table—and
even a Revereware
coffeepot—carry
out the period look.*

IN ANOTHER VERSION of open storage, big glass jars are hand-lettered to identify their contents—in French—while simple trays hold cutlery. On the wall, assorted strainers, steamers, and colanders are surprisingly decorative.

IT COULD BE A KITCHEN IN PROVENCE: the use of separate "unfitted" furniture units of natural pine instead of matched wall and base cabinets gives this work space the feeling of a European farm kitchen. Nice touches include herbs strung on bamboo rods, as well as jugs and jars filled with utensils and food staples. Weathered terra-cotta floor tiles fit right in with the rustic decor.

NEATLY CORRALLING PLATES for handy daily use yet showing them off to decorative advantage, an open plate rack lends a European cottage touch to any kitchen. To the right of the rack, a glass-fronted cupboard displays more dishes while keeping them dust-free.

A COTTAGE TABLE

A BRIGHT AND CHEERY TABLE SETS THE TONE FOR A CONVIVIAL COTTAGE MEAL. When friends and family gather around a table set with linens and dishware in sunny country colors or airy whites, with flowers abloom and food fresh from your kitchen, the atmosphere is naturally good-natured.

Your table linens—tablecloths single or layered, runners, placemats, and napkins—may be vintage embroidery and lace, retro prints, checks and stripes, solid colors or all-white. Placemats may also be woven of rustic natural materials like seagrass. Surprising combinations are fun—straw mats over a printed cloth, or small guest towels used as napkins.

Dishes can be matched or mixed—patterns with solids, old with new, plain with fancy. Mismatched pieces can be loosely coordinated by color, theme, or repeated shape.

CENTERPIECES The pride of any table, a centerpiece can be as modest as a little jug of flowers or as elegantly creative as the ones pictured on these pages. This is your chance to show off favorite decorative pieces, to create seasonal displays, and to make use of fresh fruits and vegetables as well as flowers.

SOPHISTICATED COTTAGE STYLE gets its charm from mix-and-match. Perky checks blend with retro print linens; sunflowers in snug yellow pots flank place settings of tomato-red china. An unusual centerpiece is a Wardian case—a reproduction of a Victorian container for indoor plants—holding a clutch of pillar candles nestled in moss. Above, a mini– cottage garden blooms from bottles in their own wire carrier, setting just the right informal note for a buffet table.

SUMMERS IN THE GARDEN come to mind when you set a table in
fresh whites with bright accents of lemon yellow and grass green.
Above, a three-tiered glass centerpiece bears summer fruits and
flowers. At right, silverware or even sandwiches can be wrapped
in parchment and tied with twine and fresh blossoms for a
casual cottage touch.

AWAY FROM IT ALL

WHETHER YOUR TASTE runs to romantic cottage or rustic cabin style, your bedrooms are the perfect places to express it. Create a serene space with pretty linens and quilts, and with windows curtained or shaded with a light touch. Consider a four-poster or canopy bed, or use hangings to suggest one. Instead of a bedside table, enlist a diminutive chair, a painted flea-market bookshelf or end table, or a small trunk. ❦ Make a little sitting area with a slip-covered chair, a footstool, and a floor lamp. Provide a soft rug to snuggle bare feet on uncarpeted floors; or use carpeting in a light hue to keep the look casual and uncluttered. ❦ In bathrooms, it's easy to convey cottage style with clawfoot tubs and beadboard wainscoting. But even without these, you can achieve the look you're after with

details such as gauzy curtains or fabric skirts around sinks and counters. Add old-fashioned shelves, small tables or stools, or a vintage mirror, and use baskets to hold bathing supplies.

PEACEFUL ELEGANCE is the watchword in a bedroom furnished in beautifully spare style. Awash in light from a minimally curtained window, the bed looks cool and inviting covered in white. A fall of white cotton is threaded behind the headboard, supported by brackets—an effective way to soften the look of a contemporary bed. The night-stand and decorative accents "ground" the ethereal scene with earthier color.

THE FRENCH INFLUENCE is the source of this bedroom's serene sophistication. The handsome painted cane bedstead is graced with a lovely French quilt; the vintage sky-blue nightstand is French, too. The two vintage bedside lamps were quite a find—turning a crank on their backs operates them as music boxes!

A DELICATE CANOPY of cotton netting dresses a simple bed with understated feminine charm that's just right in this seaside cottage setting. White bed linens with just a hint of blue carry out the soft, understated style. A handsome vintage mirror acts as a kind of headboard while amplifying the lovely natural light reflected in white solid-board wall paneling.

DELICATE HAND PAINTING in Easter-egg hues makes this young girl's bed a fantasy fit for a storybook cottage. Lifelike little birds perch on the charming finials of the shapely headboard; bed linens carry out the color palette of soft blue, peach, moss green, and cream. "To market, to market" goes a whimsical wooden pig hanging above the bedside table.

KIDS AND THEIR FURRY FRIENDS love a high four-poster bed piled with a puffy plaid duvet—fun to climb up into, and the perfect place to hang your hat. The utter simplicity and flexibility of this room's decor make it easily adaptable to changing tastes as children grow up. Classic furniture like this is ageless, and linens are easily swapped for new styles.

INSPIRED BY THE BRIGHT HUES of the Caribbean, this guest bedroom gets its lively vacation-cottage look from a mix of plaids and prints in reds, greens, and yellows. Salvaged shutters and an old icebox used as a nightstand add appealing quirkiness. Gauzy curtains blown by breezes through the French doors enhance the room's relaxed tropical-island feeling.

BELIEVE IT OR NOT, *this cheery master bedroom used to be a garage. Skillful conversion and imaginative decorating have turned it into a camp-style retreat, as proclaimed by the hand-crafted sign above the bed. Against light yellow walls, a red and green color scheme is carried out in camp blankets— Beacon blankets—from the 1920s, '30s, and '40s. The striped fabric on the bed is new but blends right in. Beadboard paneling on walls and cupboard doors lends cottage style, while eclectic vintage pieces, from suitcases to a horse marionette, create a fun and very personal ambience.*

A PAIR OF BUNNY
BEDS—painted cast-
iron frames with an
antiqued finish—keep
delightful company
in a little girl's room,
conjuring up images
of Peter Rabbit and
Mr. McGregor's garden.
Soft blue-green walls
and rose-scattered
comforters reflect the
tranquility of sky and
foliage glimpsed
through windows left
uncurtained.

THE SPIRIT OF SUNSET BOULEVARD
is alive in the tableau at right, part of the
bedroom also pictured on the facing page.
Above a vintage French chest of drawers, a
glitzy Art Deco mirror reflects lamplight.
A period hat mannequin wears a fetching
chapeau from the owner's collection; a
child's toy vanity of the same vintage
makes the perfect jewelry box.

SWEET SLUMBER
*is almost assured in a
bedroom furnished in
muted shades of pink and
chocolate brown. With its
vintage painted-iron bed,
this room has the charm
of a 1930s/'40s cottage.
Mirrors, including a
French antique one with
Venetian glass, help
open up this small room
by reflecting light from
several vantage points.
An old embossed-tin
ceiling tile, hung on
the wall, adds an
architectural quality.*

**A DISTINCTIVE ROUND
BEDSIDE TABLE** *carries
out the 1930s/'40s period
look of this bedroom. On the
tabletop next to a vintage
glass bed lamp, a few
simple objects—including
an Art Deco ceramic vase
holding a single hydrangea—
carry out a seashell theme.
Propping a small picture
against the wall makes a
nice, casual touch.*

SOFT YET SOPHISTICATED—
*that's the French country look chosen
for this young girl's room, and it just
happens to be in keeping with the
decor throughout the house. The color
scheme—butter yellow, soft green,
raspberry, and cream—is expressed
in a mix of Provençal-style fabrics and
striped wallpaper. French-style furniture
was hand-painted to coordinate.
Layered window valances are tied to
decorative iron brackets.*

A DREAM BEDROOM *for two sisters
has a serene, muted color scheme
of blue and white. Folded over fringed
white chenille spreads, matching star
quilts and pillow shams set out the
colors on the four-poster twin beds.
Light blue polka-dot sheers frame
the wide windows; blinds filling the
expanse provide light control.*

AN ALABAMA BUCKAROOS' bedroom comfortably houses three brothers in fine Western style. The boys' clever mother hand-painted the "log" walls and created the curtains from flannel blankets, grommeted and tied to an iron rod with strips of leather. Three twin beds feature horse-and-cowboy fabrics combined with ticking.

THAT RAH-RAH SPIRIT sure perks up this pair of beds! The spreads are vintage wool felt pennants stitched together—from Midwest schools on the left bed, California cities on the right. In between, a circular table-cloth features still more pennants. Today's sports fans might want to adapt the idea to demonstrate their own team allegiances.

AN EXQUISITE
etched-glass door,
salvaged intact from a
Midwestern farmhouse,
hints at the unique style
of the lovely, light-bathed
bathroom within.
Glimpsed on the wall,
an old Mexican wood
santo graces the top
of a weathered cabinet
beneath a romantic
crystal chandelier.

*THE AIR OF ROMANCE from a
bygone era is perfectly conveyed in the
pairing of a new pedestal sink with
the graceful oval of an antique mirror.
A small lamp enhances the scene's
old-fashioned charm, and a marble
birdbath is just the right container
for soaps or sponges.*

FORMING A PERFECTLY HARMONIOUS PICTURE, *the wooden cabinet, wicker chair, and faux-bamboo table bearing flowers lend a feeling of comfortable intimacy to the bathroom. The wonderful antique mirror with built-in shelf—probably part of an old washbasin from a public bathroom—still bears its original plaque, advising "Don't drink the water."*

IN A RUSTIC COTTAGE *bathroom, found objects from nature grace an appealing distressed table, demonstrating how a few simple touches can lend style to the humblest space. Quiet hues of blue and green emphasize the connection to nature. Blue-toned mason jars are clever containers for bathroom essentials.*

APPLE GREEN PAINT *is a bold but effective choice for this tiny powder room. Colors and decor motifs bring to mind brilliantly hued tropical fish—an apt reference in this casual Florida beach cottage. Note the painted polka-dot flowerpot for holding a magazine, the hand-painted mirror frame, and the bright spotted hand towels.*

CLASSIC TOUCHES abound in the quietly elegant bathroom shown at right and below. The owners created the lovely paint effects, which include subtly colored walls (accomplished using special brushes and hand-mixed glaze) and gilt stenciling around the archway and window. Other touches of gilding appear in the architectural detail pieces on either side of the arch and in the frames of the ornate mirror (right) and artwork (below).

A TIMELESS LOOK has been created here using a mixture of old and new. Surprisingly, the pedestal sink and clawfoot tub, the wicker chair, and even the medicine cabinet are all new pieces. The pretty wooden chair in the alcove is a French antique.

THE ULTIMATE
in romantic old-
fashioned charm, this
bathroom features
wallpaper in a toile
design (like the fabric
of the same name)
depicting French
country scenes. A
sink skirt, curtained
cabinet doors, and
lacy towels keep
the look soft and
feminine; generous
use of pure white
makes it fresh
and inviting.

TOWELS THE COLOR OF FADED ROSES are right
in keeping with the gently aged look of a bathroom
done in shabby-chic style. A piece of vintage molding
furnished with hooks makes the perfect towel rack
above a nicely balanced display featuring an oval
mirror and a long, narrow framed print. An authentic
distressed cabinet contributes to the look.

THIS SUNNY BATHROOM was designed to "grow" with the kids who use it. Rubber duckies, a whale rug, and personalized towels are fun for the little ones right now. Later on, the yellow-and-blue checkered tile wainscoting and the simple white cabinets can go sophisticated when different accessories are used.

BLUE AND YELLOW bring a special garden charm to the spacious bathroom below. Balloon shades and a sink skirt sport a cheerful floral print; using lattice to enclose the tub is an original garden-style touch. Note the floral fabric accenting the chair, lining the basket used to hold towels, and even trimming a bath mat hanging over the tub.

THE ART OF DISPLAY

SOMETIMES OBJECTS THAT CHARMED US IN A SHOP DON'T LOOK AS INTERESTING ONCE WE GET THEM HOME. The reason: artful presentation. Savvy shop owners and decorators use a few simple tricks to display objects for maximum appeal. You can use the same principles.

LAYER objects for greater interest. Prop up a picture and arrange interesting objects of varying heights and shapes in front of and around it. Create height contrast by setting small objects atop boxes or stacks of books.

GROUP smaller objects according to color, function, texture, or style. A collection of antique candleholders on a mantel—or seashells on a tray—has more impact than two or three individual pieces scattered around a room.

MIX things to create lively contrast—vintage with new, shiny with matte, round and fat with tall and thin, natural with man-made.

CAPTURE ATTENTION with a single object prominently displayed—a piece of folk art or a large basket set atop a table, an heirloom quilt or tablecloth hung on the wall.

A MEDLEY OF SMALL TREASURES that might have little impact by themselves becomes eye-catching when gathered in a wall cupboard—glass-fronted or open, as shown above. Small objects on the walls around it help create a corner full of visual interest. At right, artwork and mirrors, vintage suitcases and miniature furniture are arranged with care, and a bench serves as the anchor for both wall and standing displays. Mixing shapes on the wall and varying the scale of objects enlivens the picture.

A HOST OF FASCINATING PIECES, *carefully layered from front to back and displayed at different heights, engages the eye without looking jumbled or overwhelming. In the foreground, the seemingly random placement of candlesticks, vases, and bowls—some on the table and some raised on a small shelf—makes for a pleasing picture. The eye moves easily from these toward the display cabinet against the wall, then up to the varied geometric shapes of the intriguing objects on top. The white with off-white palette unites all the separate elements into a delightful whole.*

TINY RETREATS

IN A BUSY HOUSEHOLD, or one where space is at a premium, it's important to find a spot—however tiny—that you can call your own. A reading nook, a window seat, a little corner desk, or even a converted closet can become a haven for escape and relaxation. ❦ While such a space might not have been easy to come by in the small country cottages or one-room cabins of former days, nowadays imaginative folks have developed many clever strategies for creating private nooks. Consider installing a pull-down table or desk on one wall or curtaining off a corner, or even a window seat. If you live in an older home, an odd cranny or an old pantry might become a mini-retreat. ❦ Make the most of small spaces with furnishings that have multiple uses, such as armoires outfitted as workstations or chairs that unfold as beds. Or just pull a comfy chair and footrest up to a window, pick up a good book or a lap desk, and settle in.

PERHAPS THE ULTIMATE TINY RETREAT, *this is more than a window seat:*
it's a self-contained nook that functions as a place to curl up and relax, a
mini-library (note the bookshelves), and even a guest bed. From the
Swedish-inspired colors and decorative painting to the gracefully contoured
framing and small-paned windows, it's full of country cottage charm.

A PRIZED COLLECTION of antique stuffed animals by Steiff is a delightfully whimsical cottage-style touch on a stairway landing. Creating a small scene like this, composed around a theme, is a great way to engage people's interest for a few satisfying moments in a tiny area of the house.

AT THE TOP OF THE STAIRS, this small landing has been transformed into a lovely resting place as well as a feast for the eyes. Gently worn cabinets provide storage while making the space feel like a real room. An old chest is a convenient spot to sit and pore over treasures unearthed from a drawer. Over it all, a child's toy horse from bygone days presides from atop the cabinet.

EVEN IN A TINY BEACH COTTAGE, *it's possible to find a little spot for sitting down to jot a few stray thoughts or make a shopping list. Here, an impromptu pull-down "desk"—part of a tiny shelf by the pantry closet—provides just enough space.*

IN THE CORNER OF A BEDROOM, *a prized antique English desk and chairs combine to make a lovely and inviting spot to read, write, or day-dream. Striped walls hand-painted in whisper-soft colors, antique bird prints, and plenty of garden flowers contribute to the tranquil, feminine aura in this small "corner of one's own."*

IT COULD HAVE BEEN WASTED HALLWAY SPACE, but imaginative eyes saw a place here to create a little retreat for reading and basking in sunlight and breezes. A chair of cushioned wicker, a footstool, and a table softened with a simple muslin cloth—all in soothing white—transformed this space. Creative use of wood moldings has made possible a mini-gallery on the walls.

COTTAGE-STYLE ELEGANCE characterizes this gracious mini-office. The emphasis is on comfort and feminine charm: a handsome pine desk fills the beadboard recess, and an upholstered chair stands in for the usual wooden variety. Built-in shelving offers storage and display.

SUNNY SPACES

BASKING IN WARMTH and light is one of life's great pleasures. From the old-fashioned front porch to today's stylish sunrooms, sunny spaces foster a connection to the outdoors that's an essential part of the cottage spirit. Choose furniture made of wood (like Adirondack chairs and porch swings), wicker (painted or natural), or metal wirework (garden chairs, benches, and plant stands). Include a small table for casual dining, plus side tables—or little benches used as tables—to hold pitchers of lemonade or plates of cookies. Introduce cheery color and pattern with cushions, pillows, and even shades or curtains, stitched from weather-resistant outdoor fabrics or, for protected areas, more delicate and fanciful sheers and florals. Add whimsical flea-market pieces and folk-art accents, plenty of green plants, and lamplight or candlelight for evenings. On the practical side, fabric or bamboo shades can filter out hot after-noon sun, and an overhead fan can supply cool breezes along with tropical panache.

A WONDERFULLY ORIGINAL *iron piece from Mexico is decorated with images probably inspired by milagros —tiny cast-metal religious offerings. Against white clapboard siding, it makes a perfect backdrop for a pot of blossoms. Touches such as this abound on the plant-filled porch featured on these two pages.*

JUST AS IN THE GOOD OLD DAYS, *classic white wicker porch furniture invites sitting back and sipping lemonade in this porch's vine-shaded recesses. In the corner, a whimsical artist's rendition of a potting bench, made from found pieces, holds plants and pots next to a bistro table and chairs just right for casual dining. Lace curtains hung outside the windows reinforce the old-fashioned look.*

THE QUINTESSENTIAL COUNTRY COTTAGE PORCH, this space is overflowing
with potted shrubs, topiaries, and flowers from neighbors' cottage gardens, all displayed
with great charm and imagination. A row of small pots inhabits an antique wooden
tool box; topiaries and a tub of zinnias look right at home on an old farm table,
accented with an antique iron garden piece on the wall above.

EXUDING A WARM WELCOME, this porch relies on a
favorite color combination, red and white, to set the tone.
Anchoring the picture are a classic bench, with cushions
done up in ticking, and an old wooden farm bin, now used
to store firewood. A host of pretty container plantings,
folk-art pieces, and even a wooden pitchfork give
the porch a perky country cottage personality.

AT THE FAR END OF THE PORCH *shown on the facing page, window walls partially enclose the space to create the protected outdoor sitting room below. Here, a soothing green and white color scheme dominates, with touches of red in cushions and in the brick paving that unites this part of the porch with its "other half."*

A SCREENED PORCH is essential for outdoor living in areas where bugs can ruin a good time. This six-sided charmer, located in the South, allows the owners to enjoy breezes in a woodsy setting. Stylish garden furniture mixes easily with an old trunk; a wooden window frame hung at an eye-catching angle makes a decorative statement. Plenty of green plants and flowers bring the outdoors in.

THE AMERICAN COUNTRY THEME is in evidence on this windowed porch in the selection of perky pillows on the cushioned wicker settee. A rustic bench makes the perfect coffee table.

A COTTAGE SUNROOM couldn't be any prettier than this confection in blue and pink—
and it's an apt demonstration of how to enhance a look and color scheme through the
use of pillows! The blue and pink wicker furniture is the perfect foil for coordinated print
fabrics on a bevy of pillows. Even the decorative hatboxes set out on a wire stand are
covered in mix-and-match print paper. Wrap-around windows, sparklingly clear and
left uncurtained, contribute a bright-and-sunny atmosphere.

OUT ON THE PATIO, *a cheerfully relaxed cottage feeling prevails. Touches*
of barn red appear on a window box beneath a high, old-fashioned window,
on the funky round table, and in awning-striped pillows. A classic Adirondack
chair keeps company with a vintage bentwood rocker; whimsical accents
like a twig birdhouse and an expressive little dog figure add to the fun.

BUILT AND DECORATED *by the homeowners, this pretty deck goes beyond the usual simple platform. White latticework, overhead and on the side, serves as sunshade and privacy screen. Bright striped curtains and handsome print and pinstripe pillows and cushions for the wicker furniture were all stitched from specially treated outdoor fabrics. There's even a chandelier equipped with candles.*

LACY EMBROIDERED *vintage-style linens grace outdoor chairs for a look of pure romance and luxury. Along with the ornate style of the shell-filled fountain and the "floor" covering, they create a picture right out of a Victorian country cottage.*

FROM THE GARDEN

BLOSSOMING FLOWERS AND LUSH GREENERY JUST NATURALLY BELONG IN COTTAGE-STYLE LIVING SPACES. With their lovely colors, forms, and fragrances, foliage and flowers express a direct connection between the indoors and the countryside—even if you live in the heart of the city.

Flower arrangements for cottage-style rooms are the opposite of grand and formal. Whether or not they actually come from your own garden, they should be casually assembled bouquets with a look of serendipity—as if you had randomly gathered them. You can opt for mixed bouquets or more dramatic, all-of-a-kind arrangements. Containers can be almost anything that will hold water. A row of mismatched bottles, each holding a different flower or sprig, looks wonderfully spontaneous on a windowsill.

GREEN PLANTS Living plants are a long-standing indoor tradition, imparting a fresh and lively air to a room. Showcase a traditional houseplant on a classic wicker stand, line up fragrant herbs in clay pots along your kitchen counter, or spotlight a handsome tropical tree as a dramatic focal point for your living room or entry hall.

SUNFLOWERS AND LISIANTHUS —classic old-fashioned garden flowers—acquire a little extra polish when displayed in an heirloom silver pitcher (above). At right, a vintage wicker plant stand stylishly shows off a healthy asparagus fern, breathing life into a potentially over-looked corner.

HERE'S A COTTAGE KITCHEN *overflowing with garden bounty. On the counter and table, gatherings from farmers' market and garden await distribution to their appointed places. Over the windows, a swag of fresh greenery provides a delightful, if temporary, reminder of nature's beauty. Use fresh or dried vining greens to create such a swag in any room, joining vine sections with florist's wire and then looping the garland from small hooks over your windows. At right, a much simpler touch is a cutting or nosegay in an old-fashioned mason jar set on a windowsill.*

COTTAGE
ELEMENTS

WHAT DO A CHINA PITCHER FILLED WITH COTTAGE-GARDEN FLOWERS, A FARMHOUSE TABLE SET FOR LUNCH, and a scattering of pillows covered in a French Provincial print have in common? They're all images that fit easily into a cottage setting. In this chapter, we help you define that elusive style we call "cottage" in terms of its separate components— from furniture to fabrics, from dishware to decorative paint effects. Even if your

home lacks integral cottage style, you can use these various elements to give it real

cottage appeal.

Enliven walls and floors with cottage-style moldings or stenciling. Slipcover a

comfy old chair in fresh natural linen, make breezy kitchen curtains from vintage

tea towels, and light up your evenings with glass lamp chimneys set over a flock of

candles. Little touches like these add up to loads of charm. You'll find a host of such

ideas throughout the following pages.

CERTAIN COLORS and color combinations just naturally have that cottage look. With a long history of use in country cottages, these are hues originally produced using natural vegetable and mineral pigments. Often they're a little grayed, as if by weather and time, or gentled

COTTAGE COLORS

with a touch of white into soft pastels. At other times the cottage palette is a bright and cheery patchwork of colors. When they go contemporary, cottage colors often become soft neutrals in light earth tones.

THOSE OLD-FASHIONED BLUES

Antique glass and indigo-dyed denim, robin's eggs and cornflowers—blue's range is wide. Traditional decor might feature the strong, grayish Williamsburg blue of American Colonial paneling or the soft and restful greenish blue of classic Swedish country and American Shaker rooms. Bold or soft, the time-honored blues are just right for today's cottage-style interiors.

To give your rooms a time-softened look, paint woodwork and furniture such as cupboards and hutches in soft greenish or grayish blue. To perk up a room that has a neutral color scheme, use brighter blue as a secondary color for furnishings and accessories.

BLUE AND WHITE This classic combination can lend a fresh and open feeling to any room in your home. Pair white or off-white with tender forget-me-not blue for a sweet effect; or use pure white with brilliant delphinium blue to intensify the impact of each, creating a look that's crisp and clean. Traditional blue-and-white fabrics include striped ticking, checked gingham, plaid homespun, and toile de Jouy.

BLUE WITH YELLOW A favorite color duo from European cottage traditions, blue with yellow brings to mind images of sea edged with sand, or brilliant sunshine and clear summer sky. French Provincial fabrics in this color mix will give a room immediate European cottage charm. Combine the classic prints with coordinating solids and you have your palette ready-made.

CLOCKWISE FROM TOP:
bold kitchen cabinets set off with white touches; black-eyed Susans on a painted chair; pillow colors evoking Provençal sunshine; an Amish-inspired quilt; ceramics in softened primary hues.

COTTAGE RED *takes on many personalities—in jaunty quilted valances and checkered kitchen wallpaper that mimics old tiles (above), in understated paint on a paneled door (above right), and in the glossy finish of a country bench accented with a toile-covered pillow (right).*

THE CHEERY REDS

A weathered brick wall, old barn siding, a child's vintage wagon, a worn bandanna—all have that faded red hue often associated with the country cottage look. Reds were common in bygone days because the pigments—from minerals for paint and from the madder plant for fabrics—were relatively easy to come by. Today, soft reds and rusty hues create a delightfully cozy aura combined with a sense of age.

Look for old red-painted furniture or even fragments of barn siding at flea markets and auctions. Or you can achieve the same look on woodwork or furniture using one of the faux paint techniques shown on pages 98–103.

RED AND WHITE A ripe apple on a white plate simply illustrates the bright appeal of red and white, a color pairing you'll find in vintage needlework (patchwork, appliqué,

and embroidery), 1930s print table linens (all those cherry motifs!), and some enamelware. Use red-and-white accessories—including linens and quilts—to give a room a colorful and cheery period look.

RED, WHITE, AND BLUE It's a grand old flag! The colors of the American flag are always appealing, whether expressed in the flag motif or in other designs. Use this attention-catching combination to brighten a space and provide a focal point.

RED, WHITE, AND BLUE enjoys star status in the room at left, where strong graphic elements—flag and Red Cross motifs— stand out against a solid blue wall. Below, that most American of fabrics, blue denim, makes its appearance in a slipcover, accented with a red-and-white pillow. Above, a folk-art birdhouse sports its own miniature flag.

TIP: USE BRIGHT RED SPARINGLY, AS AN ATTENTION-GETTING ACCENT TO GIVE ANY ROOM A PICK-ME-UP.

SUNSHINE BRIGHTS

Bring instant sunshine into a room with yellow-painted walls—either a deep, warm ocher or yellow softened with white. Or use linens and bouquets of yellow blossoms to create a sun-splashed atmosphere. For an upbeat retro look from the 1930s and '40s, a collection of Fiesta-ware in its signature bold hues instantly sets a sunny tone. The colors of a summer flower border—orange, yellow, red, blue, and green—are repeated on vintage linens, pottery, and dishware.

For best effect, use bright colors with restraint, as accents. Just a few pieces of bright glassware or Mexican painted figures displayed on a colorful shelf can light up a whole room.

COTTAGE BRIGHTS
can go contemporary in
feeling—as in the zingy
oranges and blues that
enliven the dining area
above—or they can be
as charmingly traditional
as the oversize butter-
yellow checks used to
upholster the comfy
armchair at right.

SOFT GREENS can give cottage-style rooms a subtly updated look: witness the hues used to paint elements of the dining area at right, the wall behind the vintage grandfather clock shown below, and the vignette arranged on a shabby-chic cabinet (bottom). As these photos also illustrate, yellow and gold make excellent partners for green in cottage decorating schemes.

SOOTHING GREENS

Soft gray-greens called *terre verte*—traditionally produced from green clay—have long been used in country cottages. Paired with white or cream, gray-green is delicate, informal in feeling, and restful for the eye—perfect for cottage style. Brighter grass greens or deeper forest greens are "newer." Contrasted with white, they have a natural freshness—think of a white picket fence bordered by foliage.

Soft gray-green woodwork gives interiors a timeless look. And a touch as simple as a few green and gold pillows on a neutral-colored sofa, green-and-white striped cafe curtains at the kitchen window, or a vase of fresh foliage will bring a garden feeling into your rooms.

FRESH WHITES

Whether on the Greek islands or the American prairie, humble cottages everywhere traditionally featured interior walls coated with whitewash. In the absence of fancier fabrics, simple curtains and linens were fashioned of pale muslin or linen. To recall this fresh simplicity, do up a country cottage room in multiple shades of white and cream, or begin with white walls, woodwork, and even furniture and then add drama with splashes of color in soft furnishings and accessories. For a dreamy, romantic effect, combine white with delicate pastels.

A CLASSIC for a bathroom, white pairs beautifully with natural pine, as demonstrated in the scene at top. Shades of white are equally fresh and charming in the airy seaside bedroom at right. In an all-white room, small touches of color—like the green plates above—have lots of impact.

NATURE'S NEUTRALS

A restful, uncluttered atmosphere characterizes rooms that feature today's "new" softened neutrals. These are quiet hues that wear well over time—shades like celadon and putty, birch and khaki, biscuit and driftwood, straw and buttermilk. Create a serene atmosphere with natural linen slipcovers, bleached woods, and natural sisal rugs, then use clean-lined accessories like colored glass or ceramic pieces in brighter or darker hues to provide interesting accents.

UNDERSTATED HUES
of cream and biscuit allow the viewer to appreciate the interesting shapes and lines in the room above—the graceful window frame and pane dividers as well as the curving furniture contours. In the kitchen at left, a restful picture is created by the soft green of the sink skirt and the pale wood against white walls.

SURFACE CHARM

THE BASIC STRUCTURAL ELEMENTS of a room—its walls, floors, windows, and trim—are the stage on which you create your vision of a cottage-style scene. Perhaps you picture a kitchen paneled in fresh-painted white beadboard wainscoting, or you may envision a brick-paved entry hall at the foot of a pine staircase. The essential character of the framework elements provides a starting point for creating cottage style.

THE WALLS AROUND US

Cottages and country homes of past eras have featured interior walls of plaster-chinked logs or packed earth, whitewashed rough plaster or smoothly plastered wooden lath, grooved beadboard or elegant raised-wood paneling. Today's walls are often solid-board paneling or smooth-textured gypsum wallboard. But the way you finish and decorate this surface can transform an otherwise bland contemporary wall into one with delightful cottage style.

DRESSING UP DRYWALL To give ordinary wallboard interest, choose paints in cottage colors. Some new paints re-create old classics like milk paint; or use faux painting techniques to simulate aging, rustic texture, or other special looks—see pages 98–103. To add decorative pattern, consider stenciling or wallpaper.

STENCILING In the days before machine printing, patterned wallpapers —printed by hand—were a luxury only the wealthy could afford. Stenciling became the poor man's "wallpaper." Today, of course, we find stenciled walls charming; you can stencil your walls with anything from a border to an all-over motif, from floral and geometric images to lettering (for more about stenciling, see pages 104–105).

WALLPAPER For instant country cottage style, choose from a treasure chest of wallpaper colors and patterns, from traditional designs to textured papers that can mask imperfections in walls. To expand wallpaper's appeal, take advantage of coordinating borders, paints, and fabrics offered by manufacturers.

CLOCKWISE FROM TOP: stenciled motif on painted drywall; Gothic-inspired window set in painted paneled-wood wall; decorative bracket; plate rail used for display; dainty bedroom wallpaper.

THE WARMTH OF WOOD Whether as rustic log walls or smooth paneling, wood gives a room warmth and substance as well as cottage flavor. Solid-board paneling, applied either vertically or horizontally, offers a range of looks from the natural informality of knotty pine to the old-fashioned charm of beadboard.

You can panel an entire wall or create a dado that covers the lower portion—a technique often used for beadboard. Framed and paneled walls, like those favored by wealthy homeowners in Colonial Williamsburg, tend to present a more refined, sophisticated look.

Purchase wood paneling, or try this trick: attach paneled doors to walls horizontally to create instant wainscot paneling. You can have fun searching salvage yards for handsome old raised-panel doors to strip and paint.

Leave paneling natural with only a sealer applied, stain it, or choose from an almost limitless palette of colors and textures to paint it (the best option for damaged or budget grades of paneling).

FRAMED-AND-PANELED walls (above) give rooms an air of sophistication often associated with American Colonial style. At right, beadboard paneling has a more informal cottage look, especially when it is applied as a dado covering the lower half of a wall.

ANTIQUE OR RECYCLED
*board panels automatically
confer countrified charm, but
staining or special painting
techniques can mimic the
look on new wood. At left,
boards are subtly lightened
to set off the surrounding
stone. Salvaged ornamental
brackets dress up the doorway. Below, narrow board
paneling and an uncurtained
casement window create
light, bright cottage style
in a bathroom.*

LOOKING OUT If you have
attractive windows and privacy is not an issue, consider
leaving them uncurtained.
A garden view or sunlight
streaming in through bright
glass bottles on the windowsill
—unadorned windows let
you enjoy it fully. For a decorative touch, paint window
trim in a contrasting color.
Or add wooden shutters for
country cottage style and
optional privacy. (For other
window treatments, see
page 114.)

ARCHITECTURAL TRIM

Call it trim, moldings, or woodwork: we may not consciously notice these elements, but they play a big role in establishing a room's character. That's good news, because it means that just by adding interesting trim or by painting existing trim, you can add lots of personality with relatively little effort and expense.

Simply replacing skinny, undistinguished baseboards with deep ones like those shown below can make a big difference. Or give a space immediate cottage character by adding one or two of these molding pieces:

☙ CROWN MOLDING encircling a room where the walls meet the ceiling

☙ CHAIR RAIL placed 3 to 4 feet above the floor

☙ PICTURE RAIL high on the wall for hanging artwork

☙ GROOVED PLATE RAIL OR SHELF for display

☙ SHAKER PEG RAIL for hanging objects both utilitarian and decorative

With any trim, you can opt for a rough-hewn, rustic look; smooth natural wood; or a stain or paint, perhaps contrasting with your wall color.

TIP: GO CREATIVE, GARDEN STYLE, BY ATTACHING DECORATIVE WOOD GARDEN TRELLISES TO INTERIOR WALLS. THEY CAN BE PAINTED ANY COLOR, AND THEY MAKE GREAT DISPLAY SPOTS FOR ARTWORK OR EVEN SMALL POTTED PLANTS ATTACHED WITH HOOKS.

MOLDING takes many forms. Above, a plate rail supported by wood brackets neatly caps a beadboard dado and provides handy display space, while a simple crown molding defines the meeting of wall and ceiling. At left, a cabinet featuring a European-style plate rack is topped by a specially milled ornamental cornice. Below, extra-wide molding has been cleverly put together as a frame to showcase a favorite work of art.

SIMPLICITY AND PURITY OF LINE are hallmarks of traditional Shaker building and furniture style. On the facing page, practicality and beauty blend seamlessly in simply detailed baseboards and trim painted classic "Shaker blue." Peg rails are positioned both high and low on the walls, ready to neatly organize everything from hats to brooms; they could as easily display baskets and other decorative items.

STYLE UNDERFOOT

Floors in most cottage-style homes look best left bare, with perhaps a few well-placed rugs for warmth and softness. Wood floors are timeless cottage classics, whether they're standard board width or wide- or random-plank, constructed of oak, birch, maple, or even softer pine. If you have a mellow old hardwood floor in good condition, count your blessings! If your floor isn't in such good shape or you just want a new look, turn it into a real asset by staining, pickling, or painting it or by stenciling on geometric patterns or a border. (For various decorative painting techniques, see pages 98–105.) You can even paint on a faux floorcloth, as shown above.

If you don't already have a wood floor, some kinds of prefinished wood flooring now available can be installed directly over concrete or tile. Some of these floorings make good do-it-yourself projects.

BOTANICAL designs bloom on a hand-painted hardwood floor (above right), while a floorcloth—also hand-painted—sports a butterfly (above). Floorcloths are typically painted on canvas and sealed with water-based polyurethane so they'll wipe clean. For a different cottage look, you can stencil, paint, or stain a hardwood floor in a geometric pattern, as shown at right.

MORE OPTIONS Stone has been the flooring of choice for many cabins and outbuildings in the United States and Europe. In the Mediterranean tradition, terra-cotta or glazed ceramic tiles offer coolness as well as good looks underfoot. If your decor is rustic or reminiscent of Provence, Greece, or Spain, stone or ceramic tile may be just right. Brick is another old-fashioned option that looks wonderful in the right setting —especially old brick mellowed to a soft red.

CREATIVE cottage-style flooring possibilities include rustic-textured concrete with inlaid 2-by-4 dividers (top left), Mediterranean-style ceramic tile (above), and a scattering of stenciled leaves on a painted and distressed hardwood entryway floor (left).

NOTHING GIVES WALLS, woodwork, and furniture a lift—and a fresh cottage air—more effectively than a new coat of paint or a treatment with stains to lend depth as well as color. Of course, you can brush or roll on a cottage color in the conventional way. But when you

PAINTED STYLE

use the special techniques shown on these pages, furnishings take on a softly weathered appearance that makes them look as if they've been in the family for years.

PAINTERLY EFFECTS

Built up using layers of paints and glazes (thinned paints) in multiple colors, the textured or subtly patterned finishes shown on these pages are applied with a variety of tools—from ordinary paint brushes to sponges to combs. For how-to help, consult the Sunset book *Decorative Paint & Faux Finishes* or visit your local paint store or home improvement center.

To learn about the additional special decorative techniques of stenciling and stamping, see "Painters' Arts" on pages 104–105.

VINEGAR PAINTING can produce exuberant cottage charm. Using your finger or almost any small tool, you paint freehand patterns into a vinegar-thinned glaze—best for smaller surfaces such as doors, paneling, boxes, and trunks.

COMBING is a country cottage decor classic, with glaze applied in a variety of colors and then manipulated using special graining combs—appealing on floors, doors, and woodwork as well as walls.

COLORWASHING gives walls an airy, informal look. Colored glaze is brushed on in broad, random strokes over a base coat of paint, producing a textured appearance that's great for hiding flaws in wall surfaces.

FRESCO COLORWASHING yields an Old World look when a more distinct texture is added to the basic color-washing technique. Base coat and glaze are applied over an unevenly textured skim coat of joint compound.

CLOCKWISE FROM TOP: a combed built-in cabinet; fresco colorwashing above distressed paneling and cabinet; vinegar painting on a wall shelf; colorwashing with stenciled chair rail; and a distressed cabinet.

COTTAGE-STYLE PAINT EFFECTS include sponging (left), pickling (on shutters and window molding below), and spattering (bottom). The shutters, against pale colorwashed walls, were lightly distressed after pickling. The misty spattered wall was created with turquoise, blue, and plum paint over a base that fades from pale blue to white as it goes up the wall.

SPONGING can create a lively flecked or softly dappled surface. Either way, it's quick and easy to accomplish with a combination of paint and glaze and a natural sponge to dab on or remove the glaze.

PICKLING creates the look of an old-fashioned cottage when unfinished woodwork, paneling, furniture, and even flooring are lightly stained with a white or tinted glaze to simulate traditional limewashing.

SPATTERING is a time-honored technique that produces a speckled appearance; you just dip a brush in tinted glaze and pull a stick through the bristles to spray a contrasting painted surface—messy but effective!

CRACKLING simulates the random cracking of paint exposed to weather or left untreated for long periods. Patterns develop as you apply a special crackling medium over a base coat, then brush with a contrasting top coat.

DISTRESSING makes wood paneling, trim, flooring, and furnishings look gently aged. Using sandpaper and two or more paint and glaze colors, you can distress either new or previously painted wood surfaces.

AN APPEARANCE OF AGING and weathering can be achieved using the techniques of crackling and distressing. Crackled white paint was applied to the brand-new door at left and then "aged" with a dark brown paint wash. The walls below were distressed using multiple coats of brown and blue paint, each sanded away before the next was added.

WHITE PLASTER between these rough-hewn beams simulates the whitewashed look of a venerable log cottage. The chair below gets its grainy, rustic texture from a spray-on speckled finish available in kit form in paint, hardware, and home improvement stores.

TRADITIONAL PAINTS

Old-time paints had distinctive qualities, depending on the ingredients used to carry the color pigments. Paint manufacturers today offer modern versions of these classic looks.

❦ WHITEWASH or limewash has freshened the plastered walls of humble dwellings through the ages. Sometimes lightly tinted but usually left white, this treatment protected walls as well as decorated them. Today you can buy special paints that copy this look.

❦ MILK PAINTS were mixed by itinerant 17th-century painters from powdered pigments, lime, and milk or buttermilk. The resulting thick, rich color was so durable that it survives in some historic homes to this day. Purchase milk paints through specialty manufacturers, or choose oil and latex paints that simulate their colors and quality.

❦ WEATHERED TEXTURE takes time to achieve, but manufacturers offer a shortcut with paints that mimic the patina of age or create other textured effects.

STAINS FOR WOOD

Stains in natural wood colors, from light country pine to weathered cedar gray to deep walnut, have long been used to bring out wood grain and lend depth to paneling, trim, flooring, and furniture. New lines of wood stains also offer a full spectrum of colors that you can apply to unfinished furniture, cabinets, flooring, and paneling. Many stains are water-based, allowing for quick and easy cleanup.

MILK PAINT, layered and sanded, transformed the bureau above, purchased from an unfinished furniture store. Stains and special paints can give wood paneling an authentic weathered look, too, as in the photo at left. Many stains, like those shown below, have a paintlike consistency.

PAINTERS' ARTS

DECORATIVE PAINTING ON WALLS, WOOD FURNITURE, AND FLOORS IS A CENTURIES-OLD ART. For cottage dwellers who couldn't afford fancy wallpapers, carpets, and furnishings, this was an economical way to add color and pattern to their surroundings—and it was a welcome creative outlet. You can use several different techniques to give your home the same charm and individuality, in your own, updated style.

Stenciling is easy—what's difficult is choosing among all the precut patterns available through craft stores, home centers, mail-order ads, and the Internet! You can stencil a border around a wall, floor, window, or door; an all-over pattern on a wall or floor; or individual motifs in strategic spots, such as above doorways, or on wood furniture.

Some stencils are single-color patterns, while others have two or more templates for multicolor designs. On walls or furniture, use acrylic stencil paint, acrylic artist's colors sold in tubes, or even latex interior paint. For floors, use acrylic paint or colored wood stains and seal your work with nonyellowing polyurethane.

Stamping is a simple way to decorate walls or small accent pieces such as wooden boxes. Use purchased foam or rubber stamps to apply acrylic craft paint or even latex interior paint, in any patterns and colors. Random or all-over effects are informal and fun—and very forgiving!

STENCILING AND STAMPING produce charming patterns for cottage decor. Paint for stencils is applied sparingly with a flat-tipped brush (above), using a "pouncing" motion that yields a stippled or pebbled effect. Stamped designs (right) can be enhanced by hand-coloring with either paint or felt-tip pens.

DECORATIVE PAINTING *in the form of murals, trompe l'oeil, and other original hand-drawn art is an exciting option if you're a good artist or can enlist the talents of a professional. Everything from walls and ceilings to chairs and cabinets is a potential "canvas" for your art.*

SOFT TOUCHES

TO GIVE YOUR HOME FRESH COTTAGE APPEAL,
what could be simpler—or more fun—than outfitting it in imaginative
combinations of fabrics? Overstuffed armchairs upholstered in a mix of
blue-and-white checks and ticking stripes, or kitchen windows curtained
in sunny French Provincial prints—these are touches that
convey an easy cottage spirit. You don't need a lot of money
or even expertise; the secret is in your choice of fabrics and
how you use them to soften and brighten your rooms.

FRESH FABRICS

For true country cottage style, choose natural-fiber fabrics—cottons, linens, and woolens. Though you may select some synthetic blends for practicality, stick with natural fibers if you want an old-fashioned cottage feel. A little fading, wrinkling, and wear will only add to their charm.

Natural fibers can be woven into a wide range of fabric types. Cotton may be a smooth-textured chambray or a puckered seersucker, a lightweight chintz or a heavy canvas—or even textile-width panels of lace. Choose rough or homespun weaves to give your room a handmade, close-to-nature look, or create a more romantic, refined atmosphere by using gauzy cotton voile, glazed chintz, and lace.

WHERE TO USE IT Fiber weave helps determine how a fabric is best used. Loosely woven fabrics are appropriate for graceful window treatments; tighter weaves, such as broadcloth or canvas, which are more durable, are best for upholstery. Lightweight fabrics are fine for pillows and other soft furnishings that won't receive heavy wear.

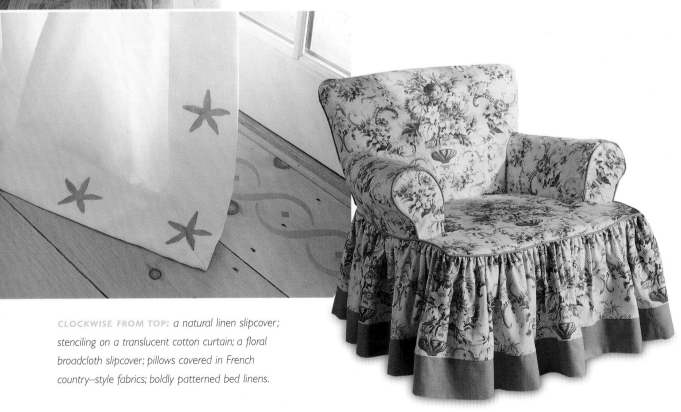

CLOCKWISE FROM TOP: a natural linen slipcover; stenciling on a translucent cotton curtain; a floral broadcloth slipcover; pillows covered in French country–style fabrics; boldly patterned bed linens.

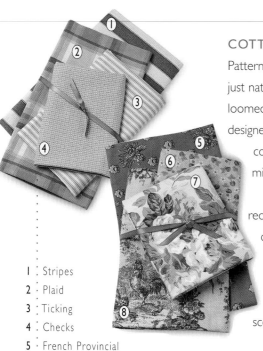

1 : Stripes
2 : Plaid
3 : Ticking
4 : Checks
5 : French Provincial
6 : Calico
7 : Chintz
8 : Toile

COTTAGE FAVORITES

Patterns that can be woven into fabric—such as plaids, stripes, and checks— just naturally have old-fashioned style, recalling the look of the earliest hand-loomed fabrics. Sturdy *ticking* material, with its woven stripes, was originally designed to keep feathers in mattresses—and ticks out. *Gingham* is a country cottage favorite characterized by woven checks (printed fabrics can mimic the look).

Popular printed choices include *French Provincial* cottons, with rich red, blue, green, and yellow patterns based on 17th- and 18th-century designs. *Calico* usually designates cotton brightly printed with dainty all-over patterns. *Chintz,* glazed for a lustrous finish, typically has large floral designs, or sometimes checks or stripes. *Toile de Jouy* (named for the factory where it originated in 1770) depicts French country scenes, printed in a single color on a plain background.

FRENCH PROVINCIAL *fabrics celebrate the intense colors of Provence, the sun-drenched region for which they are named. Here, chair cushions feature delphinium-blue figures on a ground of rich yellow; piping and tablecloth amplify the cushions' brilliant accent color.*

SOFAS UPHOLSTERED in subtle
ticking-style stripes are the perfect foil
for color-coordinated pillows covered
in chintz and other fabrics. In a kitchen,
cotton curtains in windowpane checks
have old-fashioned charm.

DON'T OVERLOOK
that most beloved of fabric
combinations—patchwork.
A patchwork quilt, be it a
bed-size coverlet or a smaller
piece suitable for hanging,
adds its own artful mix
of fabrics and can inspire the
color scheme for an entire
room. In the living room at
right, quilts add lively color
and pattern to simple white-
upholstered furnishings.

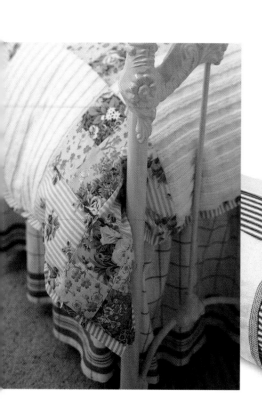

MIX AND MATCH

Cottage style encourages carefree, unstudied mixing and matching of colors and patterns. Of course, a little judicious planning can make the difference between a hodgepodge of patterns and a charmingly casual effect. Here are a few tips:

❦ MIX plaids, stripes, or checks with prints, but keep them all in the same color family—a blue-and-white toile de Jouy print and a blue-and-white gingham check, for example.

❦ VARY the scale of patterns, especially when you are mixing three or more. You might combine a dainty calico print with a bold floral and a medium-scale stripe, all in rose and cream shades.

❦ ADD solid-color accent pieces—an upholstered chair, perhaps, or some pillows—to a pattern mix to give the eye some resting places.

❦ TAKE the quick and easy approach: buy linens, curtains, and slipcovers in mix-and-match patterns offered by many manufacturers.

❦ LAYER fabrics to combine them. Top a table with a small, square print cloth spread over a floor-length cloth in a coordinated print or solid color.

CLASSIC TOILE DE JOUY and homespun gingham, united by their soft blue and white hues, make perfect partners for bed linens (left). A patchwork spread's color-coordinated prints (bottom far left) mix and match with the dust skirt's windowpane check. Ticking does the job of covering a pillow; the contrasting cover and bow add style.

LAYERED TABLECLOTHS in multi-patterned blue and white have casual cottage charm (right). Tying corners of the square cloth would also work if you are using a bedsheet as a tablecloth. On the chair below, Rover reclines against a stylish mix of bold and smaller-scale patterned fabrics.

TIP: IF YOU'RE AT ALL HANDY WITH A SEWING MACHINE, YOU CAN TURN BED SHEETS—WHICH OFTEN COME IN COORDINATED PRINTS, GEOMETRICS, AND SOLIDS—INTO CURTAINS, TABLECLOTHS, AND OTHER ACCENTS. A TABLE SKIRT OR A SMALL TABLE-TOPPER CUT FROM A SHEET REQUIRES MINIMAL SEWING.

COTTAGE QUILTS

WITH THEIR INVENTIVE PATTERNS AND COLOR COMBINATIONS, QUILTS EMBODY THE ESSENCE OF COUNTRY COTTAGE STYLE.

Even the names of quilting patterns—Log Cabin, Bear's Paw, Wedding Ring, Grandmother's Flower Garden—evoke timeless images of country places and celebrations. Some designs, like the striking patterns created by Amish quilters, have a decidedly contemporary graphic appeal. Quilting is a vibrant tradition that's being expanded to include myriad modern interpretations.

WHERE QUILTS GO Fold a collection of quilts in a display cupboard or on a shelf or side chair. (Refold them regularly to avoid permanent creases.) Drape a favorite over a sofa or quilt rack, or hang an especially stunning quilt on the wall. Use self-locking fastener tape to attach a small, lightweight one, or hang a bed-size quilt from a decorative curtain rod attached to the wall (hand-sew fabric loops to one edge, or sew on a fabric sleeve).

QUILTS are always welcome on beds, since they're pretty as well as warm, but you don't need to limit them to bedrooms. Display a single quilt or a whole collection in any room of your home. Hanging quilts over the rungs of a ladder or the bars of a rack is a wonderful way to show off their individual patterns and colors.

A PIECE OF VINTAGE PATCHWORK salvaged from a flea-market pillow sham makes the perfect cushion for a Victorian cottage—style wicker rocker. The glass-fronted cabinet shows off an enviable collection of vintage quilts while keeping them free of dust.

WINDOW TREATMENTS

Windows in a cottage-style room generally call for light and simple treatments rather than heavy, full-length draperies or elaborate styles, trim, and hardware. Cafe curtains in casual cotton prints, gauzy curtains hung from simple tabs or ties, and all kinds of light-hearted top treatments are the order of the day. Go romantic with lacy panels or cottage contemporary with shades fashioned from ticking fabric.

For top treatments, choose fabric valances on rods, or opt for truly easy swags and scarves—simply lengths of fabric gathered and draped over a rod or through decorative holders.

You may want to forgo curtains entirely if you have beautiful windows or a fine view and privacy isn't an issue; or you could use shutters in place of curtains. Bamboo blinds can be a light, easy cottage touch as well.

*COTTAGE WAYS WITH WINDOWS
include simple fabric swags draped
over hooks or pegs (top), crisp
valances gathered onto rods (center),
fabric roll-up shades (above), and
valances or curtains of sheer fabrics
or lace, like the charmer gracing
the bathroom window at right.*

TABLE LINENS

Whether your table is in the kitchen or in a dining room, you can give it instant cottage character with tablecloths, placemats, runners, and napkins. Choose perky checks or colorful florals, go romantic with lace or embroidery, or try a retro look from the 1940s and '50s with vintage printed cloths or delightful reproductions. Layer two cloths—a crisp white cutwork piece over a long, full calico cloth or bedsheet, for example. For true country cottage flair, top your table with a quilt (protected with glass or plexiglass, if necessary). Mix and match prints, checks, stripes, and plaids with solid colors for a lighthearted, casual feeling.

Your table linens can be keyed to window coverings, chair cushions, and other furnishings, or they can provide contrast. To assure a cottage look that's easy to keep fresh, opt for easy-care synthetic-cotton blends.

A SMALL QUILT that's not too precious to be washed makes a delightful alternative to a conventional tablecloth. Note how the gauzy "confetti" curtains contribute to the light, fresh look of the dining room above and pick up the colors of both quilt and dishes.

TIP: FLORAL NAPKIN RINGS—OR REAL BLOSSOMS TIED ON WITH RIBBON—ADD A SPRINGTIME GARDEN TOUCH TO THE TABLE. FOR AUTUMN, TIE NAPKINS WITH RAFFIA AND TUCK IN LEAVES, GRASSES, OR ACORNS. IN WINTER, TRY RED RIBBON AND SPRIGS OF EVERGREEN AND HOLLY.

PILLOWS AND CUSHIONS

Few elements can change the look of a room more easily and economically than new pillows and cushions. A plain flax-colored sofa becomes a focal point when you add a row of pillows in various shapes and contrasting colors; a bed invites you with comfy bolsters in country prints; a humble kitchen chair perks up with the addition of a tied-on cushion of cheery plaid fabric. If you're timid about mixing patterns and colors in an all-over room scheme, you can do it with pillows—a much less intimidating proposition.

A POUFY CUSHION and a pillow in a soft floral print add comfort and color to the wicker rocker at right. Pillows are a good way to update an upholstered chair or sofa that you can't afford to re-cover or replace. You may be able to indulge in coveted but expensive fabrics when you only need enough to cover a pillow or two.

BED LINENS

Bringing cottage style into the bedroom gives you loads of latitude for exercising your imagination. From comforter covers and dust skirts to bed curtains and canopies, bed linens are available in a tempting range of mix-and-match colors and patterns to carry out any cottage look, from romantic to rustic to breezy beach cabin. Of course, that quintessential country bed covering, the quilt, is a sure winner in any bedroom.

CREATE A ROMANTIC FANTASY LOOK by piling a potpourri of pillows onto a bed; shown here are European-style shams with lace insertion and ruffles, a bolster in a candy-striped pillowcase tied with ribbon, and assorted smaller pillows including one covered in flowered chintz.

BED CURTAINS and canopies add a distinct air of romance to a bedroom. A canopy can be the traditional arched frame, fitted with a cover of fabric or lace, or a more unstructured arrangement of fabric—even a pretty sheet—draped over an open four-poster frame as shown here. If you don't have a canopy or four-poster, you can simulate one by hanging lengths of fabric or curtains from the ceiling. Or opt for a ready-made mosquito-netting "canopy" fastened to a ring that you suspend from the ceiling above the head of the bed.

FLOOR COVERINGS

In country cottages, rugs large and small have traditionally added softness and color to bare wood, stone, or tile floors. Many old-time rugs were hooked or braided by hand, like the example below. Another charming floor covering is the floorcloth, usually made of hand-painted or stenciled canvas. For a light, garden-style touch, try a neutral-colored rug of natural sisal or seagrass. Use a patterned rug on a bare floor for an informal cottage feel, or layer a small rug over wall-to-wall carpeting.

SIMPLY DRAPE vintage table napkins diagonally over the edges of your hutch or cabinet shelves, and—voilà!—you've added a lovely and original cottage accent. You could also use vintage handkerchiefs or dresser scarves. Wide crocheted lace edging from old pillowcases will work on wooden shelving if you don't mind thumb-tacking it to the edges.

VINTAGE STYLE

For an authentic touch, nothing beats vintage linens. Tablecloths, napkins, tea towels, dresser scarves, pillowcases, sheets, handkerchiefs, and doilies from the past may feature anything from bold printed motifs in crayon colors to delicate-hued embroidery, from hand-crocheted lace to fancy openwork. Flea markets, antique shops, estate and garage sales, and rummage sales can yield wonderful pieces if you have a sharp eye.

Drape a selection of vintage handkerchiefs over a curtain rod to form a one-of-a-kind valance, or slip a pretty pillowcase over the back of a wooden chair. Hang a brightly embroidered dresser scarf as an impromptu curtain for a small window, or fashion bright checked dishtowels into a cushion. You can even tack vintage lace along the edges of a shelf, or use a tablecloth as a bed cover.

FOR A QUICK window treatment, use wooden clothespins to hang a vintage tablecloth on a tension rod or cafe curtain rod. Here, an embroidered dresser scarf has been added for a layered look. Alternatively, you could turn down the top of the tablecloth and stitch a channel for the curtain rod.

HANDLE WITH CARE Soiled pieces often can be brought back to life with careful hand-washing in warm water with a mild detergent. To keep large or heavy pieces from tearing when wet, wring out gently and wrap in towels to blot; then lay flat on towels to finish drying. Pressing with a warm iron while they are still damp will restore cotton and linen pieces to smooth crispness.

If a piece is damaged beyond repair, you can cut it up and use the "good" parts to cover a pillow or to create a curtain or placemats by sewing together a patchwork of fragments.

A MEDLEY of vintage quilt fragments makes a great composition of covers for decorative pillows (above). At left, the undamaged center square of a 1940s tablecloth gets a new lease on life as a chair cushion, framed with new gingham fabric, edged with piping, and tied with more gingham. In good condition, the "whole cloth" adorns the kitchen table below in cheery vintage style.

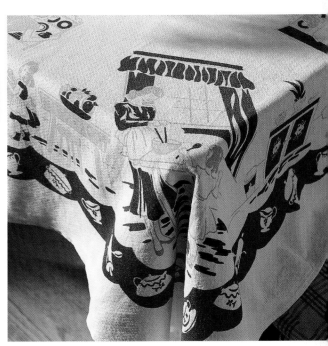

TIP: TO ACHIEVE A VINTAGE LOOK WITH NEW FABRICS OR READY-MADE LINENS, DYE THEM IN YOUR WASHING MACHINE WITH LIGHT TAN DYE TO SIMULATE THE MORE COMPLICATED TRADITIONAL PROCESS OF TEA-DYEING. SIMPLY FOLLOW THE INSTRUCTIONS ON THE DYE PACKAGE.

SLIPCOVER MAGIC

YOU DON'T HAVE TO BE A MAGICIAN TO TURN THAT OLD CHAIR OR SOFA INTO A FRESH-LOOKING, CHARMING COTTAGE PIECE.

Almost any seating—even if it has somewhat formal or super-contemporary styling—can have a cottage look when it's softened with a casually styled slipcover in natural linen, flowered chintz, or gingham checks. From ample sofas and comfy club chairs to simple wooden folding chairs, all your seating can be candidates for this transformation. You can even slipcover ottomans, stools, and bed headboards. And sometimes a "slipcover" can be a quick no-sew cover such as a bedspread or pretty sheet, draped and tucked neatly over a sofa or large chair.

SHOPPING Casual, loose-fitting slipcovers for standard-size furniture can be found through home furnishing stores, catalogs, and the Internet. Closely fitted styles or unusual shapes may call for custom-made slipcovers. For help in stitching up your own slipcovers, consult the Sunset book *Simply Slipcovers*.

FABRIC The most durable fabrics for slipcovers are firmly woven home furnishings fabrics, often called decorator fabrics. A popular "shabby-chic" look is to combine two or three coordinated small-scale prints—a floral cover with a pinstripe skirt, for example.

WHY NOT slipcover a lampshade? This one is cut from two coordinating cotton fabrics, lined with nonwoven interfacing.

SLIPCOVERS FOR CHAIRS can be all ruffles and bows, like the cotton print example above—which also lets the chair's legs show—or they can be clean-lined and tailored, like the white cover at right, which can be slipped over an ordinary straight-backed dining chair or even a folding chair.

IDENTICAL WHITE COTTON SLIPCOVERS *unite two facing sofas while emphasizing this room's fresh, light look. With their deep ruffled skirts and a fit that follows the pieces' curvy shapes, they give the "shabby-chic" aesthetic a restrained yet lighthearted interpretation. In a more traditional style, the ottoman at right features floral chintz with deep fringe trim.*

WHAT'S COTTAGE-STYLE FURNITURE? What it's not is clear—no perfectly matched sets, fancy upholstery fabrics, or stiff and formal lines. Instead, it's unpretentious pieces that are comfortable and practical, with simple lines and easy-care cushions and slipcovers.

FURNISHED FOR COMFORT

It's furniture you mix and match, combining beloved family heirlooms with handsome new pieces or flea-market finds.

STORAGE PIECES

Before the days of built-in closets and cabinets, freestanding case goods such as hutches and armoires provided storage for everything from clothing to baked goods. Today you can use these delightful pieces—vintage or new, of natural wood or painted—for their original purposes or adapt them to new uses. An old washstand might become a vanity, while a glass-fronted lawyer's bookcase or a screened pie safe could hold neatly stacked linens or quilts arranged to show off their patterns. Keep in mind that open shelving or glass-fronted cabinets look best if you select and edit their contents creatively, with an eye toward balance, form, and color. For display tips, see pages 60–61.

ARMOIRES are tall, capacious freestanding cupboards with doors and some-times drawers. Depending on how you outfit them inside, they can fulfill their traditional purpose as clothes closets or house anything from stationery supplies to your audio and video equipment. Many new pieces come already fitted with shelving specially designed to hold electronics. Vintage pieces often can be customized inside with features such as slide-out shelves and CD or DVD holders.

TRUNKS AND CHESTS, plain and fancy, have long been used for handsome storage at home as well as for travel. From rudimentary wooden boxes with flat, hinged tops to elaborately decorated, curved-lid

CLOCKWISE FROM TOP: a white-painted armoire; a vintage cabinet used as a sideboard; an antique French chicken coop fitted with a glass top; a graceful sleigh bed; seating grouped around a wood chest used as a coffee table.

trunks outfitted with drawers and compartments, they can be both decorative and practical. A simple flat-topped chest—new or vintage—can also make a wonderful coffee table or side table, or even serve as a seat.

HUTCHES and other wood cabinets have been made in a seemingly limitless variety of sizes and types, from wall and corner cupboards to dry sinks, pie safes, and chests of drawers. Hutches are large two-part pieces, usually consisting of a lower cabinet with doors and perhaps drawers and an upper part with open or enclosed shelving (sometimes with glass doors). The classic choice for storing dishes and glassware, a hutch can just as easily become a display case for sculpture or a collection.

A PAINTED and distressed cabinet (above) looks stylish in this bathroom, where an antique goat cart makes a novel towel holder. In the dining room at left, not one but two large hutches are used as a mini-museum to show off a treasure trove of quilts and dishware, with yet more cottage-style accent pieces on top.

A CLASSIC farmhouse table is a true icon of country life—the place where bread dough is kneaded, recipes are exchanged, and the family gathers to share a home-cooked meal. Here, a fine example is surrounded by an appropriately casual, eclectic collection of seats, including a vintage park bench.

TABLES

Gathering around a table—to enjoy a meal, do homework, or play a friendly game of cards—has always been a central experience for family and friends. From yesterday's trestle table in a one-room cabin to today's coffee table in a cozy living room, the table is where it all happens. Make yours a place where people want to gather by choosing an unfussy style and surrounding it with comfortable seating.

A SIDE TABLE—vintage or new, with or without a dresser scarf or fabric skirt—is an ideal place to position a lamp, display garden flowers, or set out tea.

BENCHES AND CHAIRS

In unpretentious cottages everywhere, simple wooden chairs and benches—sometimes with seats of woven rushes, or with cushions added for softness—have always provided practical seating. Here we show a sampling of beloved classics.

BENCHES—the most basic of seats—are hard to beat for versatility. Use a backless bench as a side table or even a nightstand, set one in front of the fireplace, or pull one up to a dining table. Choose benches with backs for seating in either rustic or refined style, made of painted or natural wood, or of twigs or metal. Bring a vintage park bench or garden bench indoors for a lighthearted touch.

ROCKING CHAIRS range from the simple to the sophisticated—including that 19th-century invention, the glider rocker. Conjuring up images of grandmothers and babies, of winter firesides and summer porches, the rocking chair is perhaps more ubiquitous and more beloved than any other piece of furniture.

THE WINDSOR CHAIR, with its graceful spindled back and broad seat, has been copied endlessly since it evolved in 17th-century England—named, perhaps, for its use on the grounds of Windsor Castle. A Colonial American standard, it has been adapted into everything from side chairs to rockers to benches.

ANTIQUE AND VINTAGE CHAIRS and benches never go out of style for cottage decor. The old-fashioned rocker above is a classic on a porch, while the Windsor chair at right is elegant without looking overly formal. At top, a one-of-a-kind bench looks charming with its original blue paint.

LADDERBACK CHAIRS have a clean, simple design often associated with those master furniture makers, the Shakers—but they are also characteristic of other styles, including French Provincial. Painted or plain, with wood or rush seats, with or without rockers, these sturdy chairs fit into any cottage decor.

WICKER FURNITURE, a front porch staple since the mid-1800s, lends a garden feel to indoor rooms as well as to porches. Leave it natural or paint it, with cushions covered to suit your fancy. Vintage wicker can be pricey, but lovely reproductions as well as more contemporary styles are universally available.

GARDEN CHAIRS let you extend the casual, open atmosphere of the garden into your rooms. Old favorites like Adirondack chairs or bistro chairs, painted or left with a weathered patina, are perfect for blending cottage style with today's trend of bringing outdoor furniture indoors.

FURNITURE WOVEN OF WICKER or other natural fibers —like the chair and ottoman above—has moved from the porch into the living room. The antique French wire chair at right is another example of garden furniture now at home indoors. At top right, the ladderback chair is an American classic.

THE SIMPLE,
*graceful lines of an
iron bedstead always
have old-fashioned
charm, either paired
with luxurious ruffles
and lace, as shown
here, or outfitted with
more tailored bedding.
Upholstered furniture
like the chair-and-a-half
below—countrified
with a mix-and-match
blend of prints—is the
ultimate in comfort.*

BEDS

A cottage-style bed can be anything from a simple white-painted wood frame to an iron bedstead or a romantic four-poster. What gives it a "cottage" look is the style of the bed linens, pillows, and canopies or bed curtains. For a look at more beds, see pages 44–53; for more about bed linens, see pages 116–117.

UPHOLSTERED PIECES

Early cottages and country homes didn't indulge in upholstered furniture—a luxury available only in the grand houses of the wealthy. Nowadays, though, we can all sink into the cushy comfort of an upholstered sofa or chair and put our feet up on an ottoman. Upholstered pieces can have a cottage look as long as their lines aren't stiff and formal or ultra-contemporary. If existing chairs and sofas are in good shape, simply slipcover them to acquire cottage style.

TIP: UNFINISHED FURNITURE IS LESS EXPENSIVE THAN ITS FINISHED COUNTERPART YET OFTEN OFFERS CLASSIC COTTAGE STYLING. GIVE UNFINISHED PIECES INDIVIDUAL FLAIR WITH DECORATIVE PAINTING, OR DRESS THEM UP WITH STENCILED DESIGNS.

DRESS-UPS

In these days of shabby-chic style, a little rust on a vintage garden chair or peeling paint on a wooden chest of drawers only adds appeal. But if you want to dress up an aging piece—and are willing to strip, sand, and prime as needed—here are a few ideas:

🌷 PAINT your wood or metal piece in a fresh color keyed to other elements in your room.

🌷 GIVE an old wood piece a new look by using a special painting technique such as spattering (see pages 98–105).

🌷 REPLACE old or non-function-ing

hardware with new, vintage, or reproduction hardware, such as the examples shown above.

🌷 COVER panels of cabinet or cupboard doors with cottage-style wallpaper or fabric; using fabric adhesive makes this an easy project.

🌷 GIVE a chair a new lease on life with a slipcover or an attractive tie-on or button-on cushion.

CLEVER RENOVATION gave this dated maple hutch a European cottage look. Over undercoats of coral and yellow, a green top coat was "aged" with a kitchen scrubber sponge. The doors' centers were replaced with wire mesh backed with fabric panels.

SALVAGED TREASURES

AN ORNATE WIRE BIRDCAGE MISSING ITS BOTTOM TRAY, A WOODEN BOWL WARPED BY AGE—these are the kinds of finds that gave rise to the observation that "one person's trash is another's treasure." Whether you spot them at a neighbor's garage sale or a salvage yard, the charm of such items is often in the eye of the beholder. And sometimes it's all a matter of how you use them. The birdcage becomes a kind of bell jar for a small sculpture, or the bowl joins other old wood pieces on a smooth slate sideboard.

TREASURE HUNTING *Garage sales* and *estate sales* are held in residential neighborhoods—and the older the neighborhood, the more likely it will yield vintage pieces. *Flea markets* are organized gatherings of dealers—often with an admission fee—selling everything from auto parts to fine glassware. Polite bargaining is the name of the game at both garage sales and flea markets. Sometimes you can get better deals when buying several things at once, or at the end of the day—if the item you want is still there.

Salvage outlets "rescue" parts of old structures, from wooden columns to glass doorknobs. To incorporate your finds into structural situations—as exterior windows, for instance—you'll need an understanding of building techniques and codes, or the help of a professional.

At any of these places, look carefully for flaws and needed repairs before you buy. When you've bought it, it's sold!

AN OLD FRENCH fish-market cabinet is now an eye-catching island in this kitchen. Above, a hat rack created from distressed molding and doorknobs displays vintage accessories with salvage style.

WITH A LITTLE DARING and lots of creativity, you can bring
together "found" furniture and scattered odds and ends to
make something truly wonderful, as the lavish bedroom
above beautifully illustrates. A single piece can be fun to
rework, too; the orphaned wooden cabinet door in the inset
photo, turned on its side and decoupaged, was supplied
with a row of hooks to make a one-of-a-kind rack for coats and hats.

COTTAGE ACCENTS

EVEN THE MOST BASIC ROOM takes on a cottage feeling when you accessorize it with decorative elements that express the lighthearted cottage aesthetic. Use the things you love—the old farm basket found in a village shop, whimsical bookends unearthed at a flea market—to express your own unique version of cottage style. New or old, pristine or funky, your accents should hold meaning or memories for you as well as being interesting in their own right.

IRRESISTIBLE COLLECTIBLES

Whether your passion is antique toys, seashells, or straw hats, a collection can become the centerpiece of a room's cottage look. A collection may begin with a family heirloom or a gift, or with something you discover while traveling or while poking around in a shop specializing in handicrafts, antiques, salvage, or wonderful—well—"junk." You may specialize in a broad category (wooden garden whirligigs, perhaps, or milk glass) or a narrow one (like Log Cabin quilts); or a particular motif, such as hearts or sunflowers, may guide your selections. What's important is that your collection reflect your own appreciation and enjoyment. Displayed to decorative effect, it will provide a charming and very personal focal point.

WALL ART

Whether you feature one piece or a whole collection, cottage accents displayed on a wall make a quick and easy decorating statement. You can certainly begin with artwork, signs, or plaques meant to be hung. But you can also have fun hanging plates, trays, spoons, tools, baskets, hats, quilts, game boards, sections of decorative fencing and latticework, architectural fragments, and old windows! Group items with regard to shape; to find the best arrangement, tape up pieces of paper cut to the sizes and shapes of your objects. Find interesting places to display things: position a road sign or a canoe paddle over a doorway, or hang plates around a small, high window.

CLOCKWISE FROM TOP: *a display of prized yellowware; a dramatic grouping of colorful ceramics; whimsical handmade folk art; antique carousel horses and a vintage quilt; baskets paired with a weathered drop-leaf table.*

BASKETS

Fashioned by hand through human history in nearly every culture, baskets are almost guaranteed to give a country cottage feeling to any space, be it a staircase landing, a kitchen counter, or a fireside. Use baskets for storage or as wastebaskets, turn one upside down to make a lampshade, or line an oblong basket with plastic and florist's foam to hold flower arrangements.

GLEAMING vintage glazed-pottery jugs and pitchers make a stunning display atop a sideboard; the painting enhances the tableau. A collection of English ironstone (right) is artfully arranged with an eye toward combining shapes and lines. At top, oversize baskets underscore a tabletop display complete with an armillary sundial.

POTTERY AND CHINA

Your favorite dishware may be a full set of matched china that belonged to your grandmother or an eclectic collection of pitchers from here, there, and everywhere. Either way, you can show it off as an integral part of your cottage decor. China—hard-fired, glazed, and decorated —runs the gamut from delicate bone china to hardworking ironstone. Pottery often has a more rustic personality yet can be sophisticated in form and decoration. Many people are passionate about a particular make or style of pottery; others like to collect a single form—teapots, maybe—from many makers, or choose pieces by color or design motif.

FOLK-ART DELIGHTS

The definition of folk art is fluid, but in country cottage context it usually means everyday arts and crafts. Made by hand either for practical purposes or as embellishment, folk-art objects are individual and unsophisticated in design rather than self-consciously artistic—though many "primitive" pieces from the past are now considered high art. Folk art often features common motifs, like apples, stars, or sunflowers; a stylized tulip, for example, appears repeatedly on Pennsylvania Dutch furniture. Folk-art encompasses anything from hand-carved furniture to garden whirligigs, from buttons to paintings—but however you define it, it lends charm and individuality to a cottage decor.

A HANDCRAFTED ceramic rooster makes a delightful wall ornament (top); a whale-watcher weathervane emphasizes a seacoast home's sense of place (right); and a brightly painted model windmill supplies naïve folk-art charm.

TIP: ENLIST COTTAGE ACCENT PIECES AS PRACTICAL STORAGE. BASKETS CAN HOLD FIREPLACE KINDLING OR CUTLERY AND TABLE NAPKINS. POTTERY PIECES AND GLASS VASES, BOTTLES, AND JARS—VINTAGE OR NEW— MAKE FINE CONTAINERS FOR MYRIAD SMALL THINGS LIKE KITCHEN HERBS OR BATH PRODUCTS. USE YOUR IMAGINATION!

DISPLAY, COTTAGE STYLE

One hallmark of casual cottage style is artful mixing of varied elements to catch the eye and offer a bit of the unexpected. Get creative by using a vintage object for a purpose not originally intended. A collection of painted wood checkerboards becomes a striking graphic wall display, or a child's step stool does duty as a plant stand.

Grouping like objects gives your treasures the greatest visual impact, especially if the individual objects—like the vintage bottles shown at left—are small or inconspicuous on their own. Or you can group items by color (such as blue-and-white dishware) or by materials or surface textures (like the glazed earthenware jugs shown on page 134). For additional display tips, see pages 60–61.

ANTIQUE BLUE GLASS CONTAINERS benefit from being grouped on a silver tray in front of a window, where the light brings them alive. Hanging the picture on the window frame makes an effective backdrop.

A RICH CLUSTER of accent elements—on wall, tabletop, and floor—is united in the room below by an overall floral motif and a soft pastel palette.

AN UNCLUTTERED approach to display features just a few carefully selected, closely related objects—as demonstrated here with a nautical theme (right). Note the use of twisted raffia as a curtain tieback—simple, and in perfect harmony with the little tabletop scene.

SEASONAL ACCENTS

The fall and winter holidays are opportunities to add special festive accents to your cottage-style decor. Create your own autumn harvest celebration with a centerpiece, wreath, or mantel display that shows off ruddy leaves and winter berries, dried seed pods and sculptural twigs, plump pumpkins and shiny gourds. Bring out your family's favorite Yuletide treasures— beloved old toys, that folk-art Santa or the carousel horse purchased at auction, your collection of angel ornaments or nutcrackers. Hang paper snowflakes in the window, tie red ribbons onto an everyday collection, and fill your house with the spicy aroma of evergreens and the glow of candlelight.

A BRIGHT BLUE HUTCH is an unusual and exciting stage on which to present a little holiday drama—here, a chorus of potted amaryllis and votive candles. Seasonal greens and berries frame the scene.

COUNTRY LIGHTS

IF YOUR VERSION OF COTTAGE STYLE HAS A COUNTRY FLAVOR, YOUR CHOICE OF LIGHTING CAN CREATE A COZY, WELCOMING COUNTRY ATMOSPHERE.

You'll want fixtures and lamps that are the opposite of high-tech in style yet deliver enough light to brighten your rooms efficiently. For the ultimate in cozy intimacy and old-fashioned charm, light candles or perhaps oil lamps or a pierced tin lantern during the evening hours.

While built-in indirect fixtures, recessed ceiling fixtures, and strip lighting are important to a successful overall lighting scheme, it's the decorative and portable fixtures that may do the most to set a room's style. Wired-in fixtures are available in myriad styles that say "country," from chandeliers to lantern-type wall fixtures. Lamps—both bases and shades—come in an even wider range of styles, from one-of-a-kind handcrafted pieces to mass-produced ones with great rustic flair.

IN THE DAYS before electricity, glass hurricane lamps provided protection against fire and ensured steady light shielded from breezes. Today we like to use them because they look so pretty and shed such soft, pleasing light. A collection of lovely old and new lamp chimneys, minus the bases, can be used to enclose candles set on plates or in conventional candle holders (above). Or you can opt for a real vintage oil or kerosene lamp, like the one at right; just be sure to keep the wick properly trimmed to prevent smoking.

THE RIGHT LIGHTING for a country-style cottage should look interesting and attractive
during the daytime as well as at night. The lamp shown above has a base created from
a vintage tin container and a pleasingly shaped shade—it's part of the decor even when
not lit. A row of antique finials and industrial-hardware stars atop half-shutters makes
for an eye-catching silhouette against the still-light sky outside. At right, antique wooden
spools used as candle holders make attractive accents, day or night.

Countless companies and shops, fairs and flea markets nationwide showcase cottage-style furnishings and accessories. We list a small sampling; for more, check your local newspapers and phone directory, the back pages of country and cottage decorating magazines, and the Internet. In the following

RESOURCES

listings, national chains mingle with local shops and online businesses; Internet access often blurs the distinctions among them. When addresses are not given, call or check web sites for retail store locations near you.

ANTIQUE SHOWS/FAIRS/FLEA MARKETS

www.acguide.com
Planning guide for antiques and collectibles events nationwide

www.antiquehotspots.com
Guide to finding antiques on the Internet and locally

www.fleamarketguide.com
Locations and dates of flea markets all over the United States

AMERICAN CRAFTS FESTIVAL
Lincoln Center for the Performing Arts
New York, NY
www.craftsatlincoln.org
June and September; displays by craft artists from around the country

BRIMFIELD ANTIQUE SHOW
Brimfield, MA
www.brimfieldshow.com
May, July, and September; huge outdoor market for antiques and collectibles

FIRST PRESBYTERIAN CHURCH RUMMAGE SALE
Lake Forest, IL
(847) 234-6250
May; drawing thousands of shoppers each year since 1949

HEART OF COUNTRY ANTIQUE SHOW
Nashville, TN
(800) 862-1090
www.heartofcountry.com
February; antiques representing three centuries of Americana

INTERNATIONAL QUILT FESTIVAL
Houston, TX
(713) 781-6864
www.quilts.com
October–November; huge show featuring new and old quilts, classes, lectures, and other events

JUNKMARKET
Long Lake, MN
(952) 249-9151
www.junkmarketonline.com
Five times yearly; cast-offs creatively recycled as casual cottage decor

LONG BEACH ANTIQUE & COLLECTIBLE MARKET
Long Beach, CA
(323) 655-5703
www.longbeachantiquemarket.com
Third Sunday of each month; as many as 800 dealers at an outdoor market

ROUND TOP ANTIQUES FAIR
Round Top, TX
(281) 493-5501
www.roundtopantiquesfair.com
October and April; three-day event featuring 400 booths of antiques and folk art

SISTERS OUTDOOR QUILT SHOW
Sisters, OR
(541) 549-6061
www.stitchinpost.com
Second Saturday in July; the country's largest outdoor quilt show, with 1,000-plus quilts

TESUQUE PUEBLO FLEA MARKET (FORMERLY TRADER JACK'S)
Santa Fe, NM
(505) 995-8626
Weekends spring through fall; Southwestern antiques and collectibles

FURNISHINGS/ACCESSORIES

THE ANTIQUE QUILT SOURCE
(717) 492-9876
www.antiquequiltsource.com
Quilts from Pennsylvania, circa 1850–1940

BROYHILL ATTIC HEIRLOOMS
(800) 327-6944
www.broyhillfurn.com
Furniture in antique and flea-market styles

CALICO CORNERS
(800) 213-6366
www.calicocorners.com
Retail stores and mail order; featuring fabrics, window treatments, furniture

CAMPS AND COTTAGES
1231 North Coast Hwy.
Laguna Beach, CA 92651
(949) 376-8474
Classic cottage furnishings

CLUTTER
Warrenton, TX
(512) 303-3055
Open during Round Top Antiques Fair; everything from French textiles to American folk art

COUNTRY CURTAINS
(800) 876-6123
www.sendcatalog.com (Dept. 10302)
Curtains, valances, and draperies

THE COUNTRY HOUSE
(800) 331-3602
www.thecountryhouse.com
Country-style accessories and decor

CRATE & BARREL
(800) 323-5461
www.crateandbarrel.com
Furniture and accessories

DUCK SOUP
160 Mill St.
Grass Valley, CA 95945
(530) 477-7891
Gifts and accessories

GREAT JONES HOME
921 Second Ave.
Seattle, WA 98101
(206) 448-9405
Vintage American and European furnishings, linens, and accessories

HEARTHSIDE QUILTS
(800) 451-3533
www.hearthsidequilts.com
Quilt kits and instructions

IKEA
(800) 434-4532
www.ikea.com
Simple contemporary furnishings

KISETSU
310 Sir Francis Drake Blvd.
San Anselmo, CA 94960
(415) 456-9070
Antiques and interior design

LAURA ASHLEY
(800) 367-2000
www.lauraashley.com
English country–style fabrics, wallpaper, home furnishings

LAURA FISHER
1050 Second Ave., Gallery 84
New York, NY 10002
(212) 838-2596
Antique quilts and Americana

LEXINGTON HOME BRANDS
(800) 539-4636
www.lexington.com
Bob Timberlake line and other furniture

LIGHTING BY HAMMERWORKS
(508) 755-3434, (603) 279-7352
www.hammerworks.com
Handcrafted period-style lighting and hardware

MAINE COTTAGE FURNITURE
(207) 846-1430
www.mainecottage.com
Painted cottage-style furniture

MOUNTAINMADE
(877) 686-6233
www.mountainmade.com
Baskets, folk art, furniture, pottery, sculpture, and
glassware by craft artists of Appalachian region

NANCY'S MAISON ET JARDIN ANTIQUES
701 San Anselmo Ave.
San Anselmo, CA 94960
(415) 457-0998
Shabby chic–style vintage furnishings, accessories,
architectural fragments

PIERRE DEUX
(212) 570-9343, (888) 743-7732
www.pierredeux.net
Fabrics and accessories in French Provincial style

POTTERY BARN
(888) 779-5176
www.potterybarn.com
Contemporary and cottage-style furnishings

RALPH LAUREN HOME COLLECTION
(800) 377-7656
www.polo.com
Home accessories and fabrics

RED AND WHITE KITCHEN COMPANY
www.redandwhitekitchen.com
Retro 1940s/'50s-style tablecloths, placemats,
dish towels, aprons

RUE DE FRANCE
(800) 777-0998
www.ruedefrance.com
French country–style window treatments, linens,
furniture, accessories

SAN ANSELMO COUNTRY STORE
312 Sir Francis Drake Blvd.
San Anselmo, CA 94960
(415) 258-0922
Antique wood furniture

SHAKER SHOPS WEST
5 Inverness Way
Inverness, CA 94937
(415) 669-7256
www.shaker@shakershops.com
Reproduction Shaker furniture and accessories

SHAKER WORKSHOPS
(800) 840-9121
www.shakerworkshops.com
Reproductions of traditional Shaker furniture
and accessories, custom-finished or in kit form

SPRING GARD'N DESIGNS
(818) 563-9766, (800) 563-5811
www.SpringGardn.com
Washable slipcovers, tablecloths, and pillows

STEVE REED FURNITURE
(510) 233-4624
www.stevereedfurniture.com
Handmade, hand-painted furniture

SUMMERHOUSE
1833 4th St., Berkeley, CA 94710
(510) 549-9914
21 Throckmorton, Mill Valley, CA 94941
(415) 383-6695
Eclectic furnishings and accessories

SURE FIT SLIPCOVERS BY MAIL
(800) 305-5857
www.surefit.com
Slipcovers to fit most upholstered furniture

TRÉMOLAT
226 Sir Francis Drake Blvd.
San Anselmo, CA 94960
(415) 457-5274
European-style furniture, linens, accessories

UNCOMMON OBJECTS
1512 South Congress Ave.
Austin, TX 78704
(512) 442-4000
Eighteen vendors with goods from mid-1800s
through mid-1900s

YANKEE PRIDE
(800) 848-7610
www.yankeepride.com
Braided, hand-hooked, rag, and woven rugs

DECORATING MATERIALS

AUTHENTIC PINE FLOORS, INC.
(800) 283-6038
www.authenticpinefloors.com
Heart pine and wide plank kiln-dried flooring

CONKLIN'S ANTIQUE BARNWOOD
& HAND HEWN BEAMS
(570) 465-3832
www.conklinsbarnwood.com
Antique lumber flooring, beams, and more

OLDE CENTURY COLORS, INC.
(574) 234-6728
www.oldcenturycolors.com
Simulated milk paints, paints in vintage colors

OLD-FASHIONED MILK PAINT COMPANY
(978) 448-2754
www.milkpaint.com
Specializing in milk paints

PLAID ENTERPRISES, INC.
www.plaidonline.com
Stenciling, stamping, and other craft materials

PORTOLA PAINTS & GLAZES
(818) 623-9394
www.portolapaints.com
Milk paint, limewash, and more

WAVERLY
(800) 423-5881
www.waverly.com
Coordinated wallpapers, fabrics, linens

YOWLER & SHEPPS STENCILS
www.yowlersheppsstencils.com
Stencil patterns and stenciling supplies

SALVAGE

ANTIQUITIES AND ODDITIES
ARCHITECTURAL SALVAGE
2045 Broadway
Kansas City, MO 64108
(816) 283-3740
www.aoarchitecturalsalvage.com
Architectural fragments and ornaments

ARCHITECTURAL ARTIFACTS
2207 Larimer St.
Denver, CO 80205
(303) 292-6012
Unique salvage items

FLORIDA VICTORIAN ARCHITECTURAL
ANTIQUES AND SALVAGE
112 West Georgia Ave.
Deland, FL 32720
(386) 734-9300
www.floridavictorian.com
Architectural fragments, ornaments, and more

OHMEGA SALVAGE GENERAL STORE
2407 and 2400 San Pablo Ave.
Berkeley, CA 94702
(510) 204-0767
www.ohmegasalvage.com
Vintage architectural fragments, windows,
fixtures, lighting, plus some reproductions

REJUVENATION HOUSE PARTS
1100 SE Grand
Portland, OR 97214
(503) 238-1900
www.rejuvenation.com
Salvage pieces in a studio setting

DESIGN

FRONT MATTER 2 *DESIGN:* Nancy Bostwick/Nancy's Maison et Jardin Antiques **3 TOP** *DESIGN:* Christopher Blake

FRESH COTTAGE STYLE 4 TOP *DESIGN:* Jane Walter and Robert Adams/ SummerHouse **5 CENTER** *DESIGN:* Pamela Fritz/Interieur Perdu **5 BOTTOM RIGHT** *PILLOWS:* Trémolat

COTTAGE ROOMS 6–7 *DESIGN:* Nancy Bostwick/Nancy's Maison et Jardin Antiques **8 TOP RIGHT** *DESIGN:* Astrid Vigeland **8 BOTTOM RIGHT** *DESIGN:* Molly English/Camps and Cottages; *BENCH DESIGN:* Steve Reed **9 TOP** *ARCHITECT:* Roc Caivano **10 TOP** *DESIGN:* Nancy Bostwick/Nancy's Maison et Jardin Antiques **10 BOTTOM** *DESIGN:* Christine Worboys **11 TOP** *DESIGN:* Joseph Paul Davis **11 BOTTOM** *TOPIARIES:* Kisetsu **12** *DESIGN:* Astrid Vigeland **13 TOP LEFT** *DESIGN:* Molly English/Camps and Cottages; *CUPBOARD AND BENCH DESIGN:* Steve Reed **14 TOP LEFT, CENTER, BOTTOM LEFT** *DESIGN:* Jane Walter and Robert Adams/Summer-House **14 TOP RIGHT** *DESIGN:* Nancy Gilbert/San Anselmo Country Store **14 BOTTOM CENTER** *DESIGN:* Molly English/Camps and Cottages **14 BOTTOM RIGHT** *DESIGN:* Nancy Bostwick/Nancy's Maison et Jardin Antiques **15 BOTTOM** *DESIGN:* Elizabeth Kirkpatrick **16–17 ALL** *DESIGN:* Nancy Gilbert/San Anselmo Country Store **18–19 ALL** *DESIGN:* Nancy Gilbert/San Anselmo Country Store **20–21 ALL** *DESIGN:* Jane Walter and Robert Adams/SummerHouse **22–23 ALL** *DESIGN:* Molly English/Camps and Cottages; *CABINET DESIGN:* Steve Reed **26 TOP** *DESIGN:* Pamela Green Interiors **26 BOTTOM RIGHT** *ARCHITECT:* Karl Golden **28 BOTH** *DESIGN:* Nancy Bostwick/ Nancy's Maison et Jardin Antiques **29 TOP** *DESIGN:* Polly Peters Design **30–31 ALL** *DESIGN:* Nancy Bostwick/Nancy's Maison et Jardin Antiques **32 LEFT** *DESIGN:* Mary Roath/Duck Soup **32 BOTTOM** *DESIGN:* Nancy Bostwick/Nancy's Maison et Jardin Antiques **33 TOP** *DESIGN:* Christine Worboys **33 BOTTOM** *DESIGN:* Shirley Jensen/Forget-Me-Nots Designs **34–35 ALL** *DESIGN:* Christine Worboys **36–37 ALL** *DESIGN:* Cynthia Featherston **38 BOTH** *DESIGN:* Jane Walter and Robert Adams/SummerHouse **39 TOP LEFT AND RIGHT** *DESIGN:* Nancy Bostwick/Nancy's Maison et Jardin Antiques **39 BOTTOM** *DESIGN:* Jane Walter and Robert Adams/Summer-House **40 BOTTOM** *DESIGN:* Mary Roath/Duck Soup **41 BOTTOM** *DESIGN:* Peggy and Clyde Turbeville **42 BOTTOM** *DESIGN:* JoAnn Masaoka Van Atta **43 TOP** *DESIGN:* Silke Solomon/ Trémolat **44 TOP LEFT** *DESIGN:* Nancy Bostwick/Nancy's Maison et Jardin Antiques **44 BOTTOM LEFT** *DESIGN:* Pamela Green Interiors **44 BOTTOM RIGHT** *DESIGN:* Karen and Shaun Burke/Bravura Finishes Decorative Painting **46 BOTTOM** *DESIGN:* Jane Walter and Robert Adams/SummerHouse **47 BOTTOM** *DECORATIVE FURNITURE PAINTING:* Gracie Knight **48 BOTTOM** *DESIGN:* Nancy Bostwick/ Nancy's Maison et Jardin Antiques **49** *DESIGN:* Molly English/Camps and Cottages; *SIGN DESIGN:* Steve Reed **50 BOTTOM** *DESIGN:* Nancy Bostwick/Nancy's Maison et Jardin Antiques **51 BOTH** *DESIGN:* Nancy Bostwick/Nancy's Maison et Jardin Antiques **52 TOP** *DESIGN:* Pamela Green Interiors **52 BOTTOM** *DESIGN:* Linda Woodrum **53 TOP** *DESIGN:* Tracey Runnion **53 BOTTOM** *DESIGN:* Molly English/Camps and Cottages **54–55 ALL** *DESIGN:* Jane Walter and Robert Adams/SummerHouse **56 BOTTOM** *DESIGN:* Becky Wright and Jean Tucker **57 BOTH** *DESIGN:* Karen and Shaun Burke/Bravura Finishes Decorative Painting **58 BOTTOM** *DESIGN:* Nancy

PHOTOGRAPHY

*Unless otherwise credited, all photographs are by **Jamie Hadley.***

Jean Allsopp: 43 bottom, 79 bottom; **Scott Atkinson:** 83 center; **Gordon Beall/Gordon Beall Photography:** 11 top; **Ralph Bogertman:** 107 top; **Bruce Buck:** 132 top; **James Carrier:** 102 bottom, 103 bottom right; **Frasier Edwards:** 111 top; **Gloria Gale/Ron Anderson:** 79 top, 112 bottom, 124 bottom; **Gloria Gale/ Bill Matthews:** 139 top; **Gloria Gale/Bradley Olman:** 104 top; **Tria Giovan:** 9 bottom, 13 bottom, 25 both, 29 bottom, 32 top right, 40 top, 41 top, 44 top right, 44–45 center, 45 right, 46 top, 47 top, 56 top, 59 bottom, 62–63 center, 68 left, 85 left, 86 top, 88 bottom right, 90 bottom, 92 bottom, 93 both, 99 center, 100 right, 101 bottom, 103 bottom left, 105, 109 top left, 116 bottom, 117 bottom left, 122 bottom, 127 top left and right, 128 top, 133 center, 135 bottom right, 136 top and bottom right, 137 bottom; **Ken Gutmaker:** 92 top, 106 bottom; **Margot Hartford:** 130 bottom; **Philip Harvey:** 59 bottom

Numbers in **bold face type** refer to photographs.

INDEX